Jeannette Yeznach Wick, RPh, MBA

Pharmacy Practice in an Aging Society

Pre-publication
REVIEWS,
COMMENTARIES,
EVALUATIONS . . .

"**A** well written book that will be very helpful to both established practitioners in senior care pharmacy as well as new practitioners. I truly enjoyed it!"

Nicole Brandt, PharmD, CGP, BCPP
Assistant Professor, Geriatric Pharmacotherapy,
University of Maryland, School of Pharmacy

"**T**his is a remarkable book that deserves a much wider audience than just practicing pharmacists. Pharmacists should read this book to help prepare for the increasing demands that an aging society will place on their services. And when they do they will find that aging is much more than a head of white hair over a handful of prescrip-

tion slips. Wick takes the oft heard, but underappreciated phrase 'the whole person' to a new level in this work. To be sure, there is content regarding which medications should and should not be taken by seniors with particular diseases, but the main emphasis of the book is on factors frequently overlooked when treating older persons—communication, exercise, stress, sexuality, addiction. Another noteworthy attribute of the book is the author's easy writing style and avoidance of medical jargon. She mixes humor with serious content in a book certain to be a useful reference to health professionals and informal caregivers alike."

Bruce Stuart, PhD
Professor and Director,
The Peter Lamy Center
on Drug Therapy and Aging,
University of Maryland School of Pharmacy

More pre-publication
REVIEWS, COMMENTARIES, EVALUATIONS . . .

"This is a compilation of background information, personal experience, and practical instruction to support pharmacists in tuning their professional conduct and delivery of advice toward best practice within a successfully ageing society. It covers a vitally necessary context of modern practice, particularly in the United States, but with some aspects also relevant to other settings. Didactic, readable, and personal, rather than strictly academic in approach, the author succeeds in addressing many of the prevalent pitfalls of ageist professional attitudes without reinforcing them. As well as useful coverage of demography and epidemiology, there are informative chapters on pharmacological dependency, cognitive impairment, and stress, that reflect the author's extensive background in mental health practice, and there are useful bibliographies and reading recommendations throughout."

Cameron G. Swift, PhD, FRCP, FRCPI
Emeritus Professor of Health Care
of the Elderly,
King's College School of Medicine,
King's College, London

✓PPP

Pharmaceutical Products Press®
An Imprint of The Haworth Press, Inc.
New York • London • Oxford

Pharmacy Practice in an Aging Society

Pharmacy Practice in an Aging Society

Jeannette Yeznach Wick, RPh, MBA

ℐPPP

Pharmaceutical Products Press®
An Imprint of The Haworth Press, Inc.
New York • London • Oxford

For more information on this book or to order, visit
http://www.haworthpress.com/store/product.asp?sku=5404

or call 1-800-HAWORTH (800-429-6784) in the United States and Canada
or (607) 722-5857 outside the United States and Canada

or contact orders@HaworthPress.com

Published by

Pharmaceutical Products Press®, an imprint of The Haworth Press, Inc., 10 Alice Street, Binghamton, NY 13904-1580.

PUBLISHER'S NOTE
The development, preparation, and publication of this work has been undertaken with great care. However, the Publisher, employees, editors, and agents of The Haworth Press are not responsible for any errors contained herein or for consequences that may ensue from use of materials or information contained in this work. The Haworth Press is committed to the dissemination of ideas and information according to the highest standards of intellectual freedom and the free exchange of ideas. Statements made and opinions expressed in this publication do not necessarily reflect the views of the Publisher, Directors, management, or staff of The Haworth Press, Inc., or an endorsement by them.

Cover design by Jennifer M. Gaska.

Library of Congress Cataloging-in-Publication Data

Wick, Jeannette Y.
    Pharmacy practice in an aging society / Jeannette Yeznach Wick.
        p. ; cm.
    Includes bibliographical references and index.
    ISBN-13: 978-0-7890-2651-4 (hard : alk. paper)
    ISBN-10: 0-7890-2651-1 (hard : alk. paper)
    ISBN-13: 978-0-7890-2652-1 (soft : alk. paper)
    ISBN-10: 0-7890-2652-X (soft : alk. paper)
        1. Geriatric pharmacology. 2. Pharmacists—United States. 3. Pharmacist and patient—United States. [DNLM: 1. Community Pharmacy Services. 2. Health Services for the Aged. 3. Pharmacists. 4. Professional-Patient Relations. QV 737 W636p 2006] I. Title.

RC953.7.W53 2006
615'10846—dc22

2006004456

To my mother, Elizabeth Yeznach

ABOUT THE AUTHOR

Jeannette Yeznach Wick, RPh, MBA, is senior clinical research pharmacist at the National Institutes of Health. She has been a practicing pharmacist for more than 25 years and a widely published medical for more than a decade. She was formerly chief pharmacist for the District of Columbia's Department of Mental Health, a large facility that provides inpatient, outpatient, and long-term care services to the mentally ill. Ms. Wick is the author of *Supervision: A Pharmacy Perspective* and is a frequent contributor to both *The Journal of the American Pharmacists Association* and *The Consultant Pharmacist.*

CONTENTS

Foreword

I shall never forget a reception I attended twenty years ago when the CEO of a major pharmaceutical company asked me, "How old do you think you would be if you did not know the day you were born?" He wanted an immediate response—no thinking about the answer! I said I felt twenty-four years old—about half my age. He then said, "That is your psychological age." Through the years I started looking at colleagues and elderly friends of my parents. Some people "looked" their age and many others "looked" much younger.

Even though society classifies anyone over sixty-five years as elderly, our bodies age at different rates. Within the pages of this book, Dr. Wick confronts the different types of problems that people have with their medications as they age and recommends ways that pharmacists can provide better pharmaceutical care. She is very sensitive to the ethical and communication needs of the elderly and provides pharmacists with insightful techniques that can be used so elderly patients will feel respected but at the same time be given the medication information and care they need.

This book should touch the heart of every pharmacist. The last step in the delivery of high pharmaceutical care is the translation of the pharmacological information into language that each patient can understand. This book contains a wealth of practical tips on how to meet the wide variety of information needs of the elderly. Dr. Wick makes it very clear that the communication needs are dynamic. Each future generation is going to have different needs because their beliefs and attitudes are molded by key events that happened during their younger years.

Pharmacy Practice in an Aging Society
© 2006 by The Haworth Press, Inc. All rights reserved.
doi:10.1300/5404_a

As pharmacists learn how to reach out in more effective ways to their aging patients, they will gain a better understanding of the psychological and social riches the elderly have . . . and which no amount of money can buy. Enjoy every page of this book as you read the humor and gain a better awareness of your patients . . . your parents . . . and yourself.

Dorothy L. Smith, PharmD
President and CEO
Consumer Health Information Corporation
McLean, Virginia

Preface

Geriatrics, gerontology, and aging were of no interest to me when I studied pharmacy in the early 1970s. The curriculum's emphasis whenever these topics were discussed was renal failure, hepatic failure, and cognitive decline. Little was done to dispel generally accepted myths about aging; students tended to believe that most people wind up in nursing homes, dementia was the rule rather than the exception, and aging was a homogenous process and, in fact, a disease. This was not and is not a problem unique to pharmacists. Many health professions suffer the same problem.

Fortunately, life interceded and changed my way of thinking. Many elders took the time to advise and guide me personally and professionally. Without them, life would have been much more difficult and less interesting. A lack of writers willing or able to write about geriatrics or aging opened a door for me as I attempted to develop a new, parallel career as a writer. (The subject may not have been my first choice, but it was my only choice at times.) In my primary practice site at one of this nation's largest psychiatric facilities, I observed that the mentally ill seemed to age prematurely, introducing the ideas of frailty and robust aging rather sereptitiously. A growing appreciation for statistics (fewer than 5 percent of elders end up in a nursing home, and many of them only stay long enough to recover or rehabilitate and return home) and language (Isn't senescence a beautiful word? Wrinkle is, too.) woke me to reality.

These experiences—the kindness and wisdom of elders, the opportunity geriatrics offered and continues to offer, the observation that aging is each person's most unique and often most beautiful experience, and the insight into aging's statistics and language—have convinced me that there is a need to enlighten pharmacists about aging. Our profession's insistence on focusing on the frail to the detri-

Pharmacy Practice in an Aging Society
© 2006 by The Haworth Press, Inc. All rights reserved.
doi:10.1300/5404_b

ment of the normal and the robust sometimes frustrates me. The other 95 percent of elders need our attention and care, too.

We can provide better care to all elders. Developing the competence to do so is as easy as acknowledging that we are not born knowing about aging, then listening to our elders. And, if the past is any indication of the future, science will help us lengthen life and improve its quality. The chapters in this book will introduce aging from a perspective that differs from the traditional. The book (1) assumes readers have a sound understanding of the basics of biology, pharmacokinetics, and pharmacodynamics taught in pharmacy school; (2) introduces some tangential issues of aging; and (3) stresses practical application of what we know.

Acknowledgments

Many people help when a book is being written, and it is impossible to list (or even remember) everyone. Forgive me if I have missed you. Thanks to Daniel P. Fragassi, Skip Hall, Mike Hydorn, Robert Keisling, Patricia Schettino, Ron Teeter, Christopher Ticknor, Caroline Wick, Dennis Worthen, Elizabth Yeznach, Guido R. Zanni. And the countless number of aging individuals who contact me for counseling and information.

Pharmacy Practice in an Aging Society
© 2006 by The Haworth Press, Inc. All rights reserved.
doi:10.1300/5404_c

Chapter 1

A Graying Landscape

In the 1960s, my family would gather in the living room during the evening to watch television in the era before cable and remote control. The adults, my father in particular, chose the program, and channel changing was a children's job. The kids (lying on pillows on the floor) dutifully hopped up to turn the dial.

From my perspective, the adults were pretty old, in their late thirties or early forties. We were once watching an absolutely ancient comedian, George Burns (1896-1996), deliver a comedy routine on the exigencies of aging; he was probably in his mid-sixties. Many of the jokes were beyond our understanding, but my parents' chuckles turned to laughter as Burns delivered line after line about growing old. They literally roared when he said, "How do you know you're getting old? It's when you bend down to tie your shoe, and you ask yourself, 'Is there anything else I can do while I'm down here?'"

I didn't get it then. I do now, having not just passed the age that my parents were then, but having come soberingly close to the age at which my father died. I rarely feel old. But during my late twenties, when I was aging simultaneously with my unborn child, I fell into the habit of asking myself, "Is there anything else I can do while I'm down here?" as I lowered my expanded girth to tie my shoes. These days, I still ask myself this question, but for different reasons.

Aging is, of course, about accumulating years. But as this story demonstrates, it is also about perspective, our own and others'. Currently, sixty-five years is generally accepted as the threshold for "elderly." This book will use sixty-five as the threshold, too, but will stress that chronological age, or the number of years since one's birth, is arguably less important than functional age, or how well one functions in his or her social environment.

Pharmacy Practice in an Aging Society
© 2006 by The Haworth Press, Inc. All rights reserved.
doi:10.1300/5404_01

Functional age is a combination of psychological age, social age, and physiological/biological age. Older adults' creative and scholarly work indicates that functionally many people aged sixty-five or older are, productively at least, still young. The most productive years for historians, botanists, inventors, philosophers, and writers often arrive in the seventh decade of life. Goethe finished *Faust* at eighty-two, Michelangelo started the dome of St. Peter's at age seventy-one, and Cervantes wrote *Don Quixote* at sixty-eight.

With people over sixty-five representing a growing section of our society, health care professionals need to have or to develop special tools for dealing with elders. Often, transgenerational communication is hampered by different perspectives, different approaches, and even different meanings for the same words. This book identifies areas pharmacists are likely to find most challenging in their work with the elderly and provides a framework for addressing these areas.

Each chapter approaches a health care issue and the associated concerns of aging America. Throughout the book, exhibits, figures, and tables are used to summarize key facts:

- *Communication,* using "good, better, best" examples, offers ways of delivering difficult or even unwelcome information in an appropriate vocabulary.
- *Ethics on the Spot* helps pharmacists deal with difficult questions that can be anticipated, and determining what information is appropriate to divulge and what is not.
- *Statistics at a Glance* lists comparative statistics in a way that makes a point.
- *Cutting Edge* describes what is at the forefront of research, and what that means in terms of availability to patients.
- *Too Late Now* describes the circumstances under which changing a behavior or adding a medication is probably not worth the effort (e.g., finasteride after all hair has been gone for years, or quitting smoking after age seventy-five if unmotivated).
- *Then and Now* compares previous treatments or approaches with those employed now.
- *The Bum's Rush,* named after a slang phrase that developed around 1910 meaning a hasty exit or forcible eviction, indicates that there is insufficient room for any additional explanation. This book can only introduce topics. You, however, can find

more information on the Internet links, in books, or from organizations that provide good quality, helpful information on the topic. You can also develop empathy for older patients by reading certain novels or watching certain movies. Where appropriate, fictional works are noted.

Let's start with Statistics at a Glance. Before looking at Exhibit 1.1, estimate the median age of the American population. Now, look at the exhibit. Surprised?

Japan and Italy are the "grayest" countries in the world, with median ages of 40.0-41.2 and 40.2, respectively.[1,2] Less developed cou-

---

EXHIBIT 1.1.
Statistics at a Glance: What's the Median?

Many factors affect a society's median age, many of them beyond our control: birth rate, mortality rate, war and diaspora, migration, influenza and other epidemics, nutrition, natural disasters, and so forth. Consider these figures for the United States:

Year	Median Age	Life Expectancy at Birth
1800	16	30
1850	19	38.3
1900	22.8	48.2
1950	28	66.1
1975	30.1	67.9
2000	35.5	74.8
2050 (projected)	40.7	82.6

The median age of our population in 2001 was greater than the average life expectancy in 1800. Clearly, the U.S. population is aging.

Sources: United Nations. World Population, Ageing, 1950-2050: United States. Available at http://www.un.org/esa/population/publications/worldageing19502050/pdf/207unite.pdf. Accessed December 17, 2003; InfoPlease. Life expectancy by age, 1850-2001. Available at http://www.infoplease.com/ipa/A0005140.html. Accessed December 19, 2004.

ntries tend to have lower median ages, hovering around 24.2 years. In terms of sheer numbers of people older than eighty, only China surpasses the United States globally. The number of people aged sixty-five or more will more than double before 2025, but the number of children will increase by only 3 percent.[3] Within the next twenty years, the picture in the United States will be more complicated as a full 25 percent of people over sixty-five will be from minority populations.

WHO'S WHO?

Each American generation's beliefs and attitudes are molded by the key events that occurred during their formative years, and the context of life becomes more important as one ages. Pharmacists should be aware of specific generational nuances, but not assume that qualities and ideas representative of a generation are necessarily true of the individual patient. Within the context of life and times, everyone develops in unique ways biologically, socially, intellectually, and psychologically.

Using a broad understanding of generational context to formulate questions, while acknowledging a responsibility to understand individual patients outside of that broad understanding, is prudent. Although the following descriptions of the different generations in the United States are broad, they outline the historical and social contexts in which successive generations have aged.

Veterans or Seniors (Born Between 1922 and 1943)

Also called the traditionalists, the silent majority, or the Matures, the 52 million Americans born into this generation are generally conservative, are unlikely to take risks, and tend to have been exposed to less diversity than their children and grandchildren.[4] The events that shaped their personalities, values, and beliefs were the Great Depression, World War II, and the Korean War. This "God, family, and country" generation respects authority, is loyal, works hard, and will dedicate themselves enthusiastically to a task or project. Approximately 74,000 members of this generation die each month.[5]

Baby Boomers (Born Between 1943 and 1960)

Also called the Sandwich Generation, 74 million children were born into this generation. More than any previous generation, the baby boomers have had a wide range of educational opportunities[4] and have been the beneficiaries of unparalleled economic growth and prosperity. The fight for civil rights, equality for women, the space program, the Cold War, and the Vietnam War shaped their values and expectations. They value youth, health, personal gratification, and material wealth.[6] They also value speed, want things now, and are highly competitive.[4] This generation is extremely optimistic and thinks it changed the world with their social activism, challenge of rules, and hard work (they define themselves by their work). In actuality, the world may have changed to accommodate them.

Generation Xers (Born Between 1960 and 1980)

The children of the boomers, Generation Xers, numbering 70 million, seem to be characterized by their reaction to the boomers' excessive, self-centered approach and high divorce rate. They are sometimes called the Misunderstood Generation, many of them having grown up in single-parent homes, necklaced with a key on a string. Influenced by Watergate, MTV, personal computers, and the Internet, they value diversity, are motivated by money, want balance in their lives, are self-reliant, and covet their free time.[4]

Nexters (Born Between 1980 and 2000)

With 81 million among them, the Nexters—or Millennials or Generation Y—represent 30 percent of our population. They never knew life without AIDS, answering machines, microwave ovens, or videos. They are brand-conscious but not excessively so, mobile, and constantly attached to some kind of media gadgetry—a cell phone, an MP3 player, the Internet, or television. This is the most educated generation of Americans yet, and they work, play, and function best in groups. They treasure the environment and have had more exposure to ethnic and sexual minorities than their parents and grandparents. They also seem in many ways similar to the Veterans—their values are conservative compared with those of the Boomers and the Generation Xers.[4]

Practicing pharmacists may come from any of these generations. Many Veterans continue to work, and the Nexters are graduating from pharmacy school and entering the workplace. Our patients also come from all of these generations, but the majority of our clientele are from the older generations. This creates a perfect environment for generational gaps and miscommunication.

ELDERS' DEMOGRAPHICS

The current population of older adults is the wealthiest in U.S. history, with the majority having income levels above the poverty line. The federal poverty line, however, is lower for individuals sixty-five and older than for those under sixty-five, so being above the poverty line does not necessarily indicate an acceptable level of income. In addition, many elders are underinsured; they have some form of health insurance but lack adequate prescription coverage.

Typical in this category are Medicare beneficiaries who must pay for outpatient prescriptions or navigate Medicare Part D, as well as members of many managed care programs with capped prescription benefits or limited formularies. Insured elders may have adequate prescription drug riders but unaffordable copayments. Many plans have multitiered copayment systems, with an average differential of $20 between tiers.[7] Although a $35 copay for a ninety-day supply of a cholesterol-lowering drug that costs in excess of $300 seems reasonable, it becomes a hardship for elders struggling on an annual household income of $15,000.

American seniors' income constraints have serious repercussions for pharmacy. When elderly patrons look for ways to stretch their prescriptions (e.g., delaying refills, ordering only a small quantity at a time, asking about drug importation), finances may be the problem. The following list notes some resources that may help:

- Volunteers in Health Care's Web site (www.volunteersinhealth care.org) provides a comprehensive list of state-level pharmacy assistance programs and contact information.

- The National Conference of State Legislatures (www.ncsl.org/programs/health/drugaid.htm) has a similar online list that features links to several states' Web sites.
- People requiring financial relief from prescription costs are likely to need financial assistance with other needs. The National Council on Aging (www.ncoa.org) operates a free online service to seniors (fifty-five and older) that contains more than 1,150 different programs from all fifty states for heating, utilities, health, nutrition, and tax relief benefits. It also lists an average of fifty to seventy pharmacy assistance programs per state.
- BenefitsCheckUp (www.benefitscheckup.org) users complete a questionnaire focused on eligibility criteria and are then presented with a list of possible benefits for which they qualify in their geographic area. Two versions of BenefitsCheckUp exist: one for patients/consumers and one for organizations.
- www.govbenefits.gov, a government Web site, lists federally funded benefits programs. The site searches for eligible benefits based on the information entered by the user.

Long-Term Care

Only about 5 percent of older adults in the United States reside in a long-term care (LTC) facility; the proportion increases to 24 percent for those eighty-five or older. LTC facilities are no longer a place just to go to die. These facilities often provide

- short-term care following hospitalization for a serious injury or illness,
- short-term respite care for families who care for ailing older adults, so the caregiving family can rest or vacation, and
- specialized care for patients who are temporarily or permanently ventilator dependent, have Alzheimer's disease, or have other specific diseases or conditions.

Generally, nursing home residents have very specific needs and are considered frail (see Chapter 4 for a description of frailty).

When dealing with elders, family members and clinicians sometimes forget that the elder is an adult. You may hear that roles reverse as parents age and that the "parent becomes the child." This is not true. Treating elders like children is inappropriate regardless of their degree of dependence or incapacitation. Chapter 3 describes optimal communication with elders.

DEVELOPING COMPETENCE

This book aims to increase pharmacists' competence in dealing with people from older generations. Pharmacists must identify various generations' specific nuances without assuming that qualities representative of a generation are necessarily true for the individual client. We have to use our understanding of generations to formulate questions to ask; this understanding does not replace the responsibility to ask questions. Patients appreciate your efforts when you try to understand their culture with skill and aplomb. A direct, inoffensive approach puts patients at ease. Smart, sensitively phrased questions anticipate issues related to the patient's gender, economic level, family status, beliefs, and, possibly, end-of-life care.

While developing an understanding of patients' cultures, we need to recognize our own. This means examining our own beliefs and why we hold them, and putting aside misconceptions. It also means realizing that in the patient-clinician relationship, the clinician is responsible for taking the lead, establishing the tone of the relationship, and reaching out to the patient. Note, however, that because you are taking the lead in establishing and directing the relationship, the patient need not adapt to your culture or make allowances for your age.

Various chapters in this book describe the aging process, communication issues, exercise, stress, dementias, and end-of-life issues. Each chapter tries to elucidate possible concerns or biases that you may have when dealing with older patients.

Culturally Competent in "Old"?

Can you be culturally competent in "old?" Know this: Today's aged population has earned its status as the most diverse age group. Owing to the four influences on development (i.e., biology, social environment, intelligence, and psychology), everyone develops differently within the context in which they live, and context becomes more important as we age. Accumulating life experiences increase people's diversity across the life span.

Elders demonstrate a certain amount of homogeneity in response to disease. Based on experience, we can identify similarities in the way people experience disease and altered states of health. But every senior belongs to other cultural groups, and any care plan must consider the patient's individual needs.

CONCLUSION

So, can you become culturally competent in "old"? The answer is part good news, part bad. Good news first: Totally by accident, you will become more culturally competent in old every day. Bad news next: People who are members of generations older than you will be one step ahead of you. Always. Your unique experiences, and particularly the experiences you seek out in order to learn more, will influence the magnitude of your competence.

What do *you* think when *you* bend down to tie your shoes? Depending on your point of view, your history, and your expectations, situations will have different meanings. When I bend down to fasten my shoes now (not always tying, since Velcro and backless shoes are in vogue), I try not to think about aging; instead, I think about multitasking, asking myself, "What else can I do while I'm down here?" Join me now on a voyage of understanding what old means today.

The Bum's Rush

- *Since 1991, the Beers Criteria (Beers MH, Ouslander JG, Rollingher, I, et al., 1991. Explicit criteria for determining inappropriate medication use in nursing home residents. UCLA Division of Geriatric Medicine.* Arch Intern Med.*151:1825-1832) have provided guidance concerning drugs that are risky for nursing home residents. In 2003, Fick et al. updated the Beers criteria (Fick, DM, Cooper JW, Wade WE, et al., 2003. The Beers criteria for potentially inappropriate medication use in older adults: Results of a US consensus panel of experts.* Arch Intern Med. *163:2716-2724). Reading these articles can help pharmacists understand specific concerns for all older patients.*

- *We all hear horror stories about nursing homes, but some residents of these facilities develop deep relationships and have meaningful existences. Try Tracy Kidder's novel* Old Friends *for a poignant description of several seniors as they enter "their last place on earth."*
- *Do you know how elders in your area are fixed for cash? Look at* Profile of Older Americans, *available at www.lifeclinic.com/focus/seniorcare/stats.asp#Income, and you may get a better idea of why they have trouble with medication compliance.*
- *This book is not intended to be a textbook. Rather, it is an introduction to senior care pharmacy and some of its subtleties. Consider registering for* Geriatrics at Your Fingertips *at www.geriatricsatyourfingertips.org/default.asp or purchasing the hardcopy of this book at the same site for more technical information about geriatric health care. Another useful reference is* Geriatric Secrets, *edited by Forciea MA, Schwab EP, Brady D, et al. (3rd ed.) Philadelphia, PA: Hanley and Belfus, 2004.*

NOTES

1. United Nations. World Population Ageing, 1950-2050; Japan. Available at http://www.un.org/esa/population/publications/worldageing19502050/pdf/119japan.pdf. Accessed December 19, 2004.

2. United Nations. World Population Ageing, 1950-2050; Italy. Available at http://www.un.org/esa/population/publications/worldageing19502050/pdf/117italy.pdf. Accessed December 19, 2004.

3. United Nations. World Population, Ageing, 1950-2050; United States. Available at http://www.un.org/esa/population/publications/worldageing19502050/pdf/207unite.pdf. Accessed December 17, 2003.

4. Zemke R, Raines C, Filipczak B. Generations at Work: Managing the Clash of Veterans, Boomers, Xers, and Nexters in Your Workplace. New York: American Management Association; 2000.

5. Ulrich BT. Successfully managing multigenerational workforces. *Seminars for Nurse Managers* 2001;53:147-153.

6. Gerke ML. Understanding and leading the quad matrix: Four generations in the workplace: The Traditional Generation, Boomers, Gen-X, Nexters. *Seminars for Nurse Managers* 2001;9:173-181.

7. American Society of Health-System Pharmacists. Providing pharmaceutical care for indigent patients: A roundtable discussion. *Am J Health-Syst Pharm* 2001; 58:867-878.

Chapter 2

The Challenge of Disease
in the Elderly

You know you're getting old when . . .

- You don't care where your spouse goes, so long as you don't have to go along.
- Work is a lot less fun—and fun is a lot more work.
- It takes longer to rest than to get tired.
- The police no longer caution you to slow down—your doctor does.
- Caution is the only thing you care to exercise.
- You wake up with that morning-after feeling, and you didn't do anything the night before.
- You stop buying green bananas.

Jokes aside, what can humans today reasonably expect in terms of health as they age? This chapter explains some of the changes seniors can expect and how health problems at younger ages can cause difficulties later. Subsequent chapters will go into more detail on specific topics not covered here.

As our demographics have shifted, so have our health care needs. The change from a high-fertility/high-mortality to a low-fertility/low-mortality demographic has had several repercussions:

- Smaller families and longer lives have meant that our society's youth are more likely to have vertical family relationships (i.e., with members in other generations) than horizontal relationships (i.e., with siblings).[1]

Pharmacy Practice in an Aging Society
© 2006 by The Haworth Press, Inc. All rights reserved.
doi:10.1300/5404_02

- With an aging society, goods and services must be weighted in favor of the older population. Elderly people are three times more likely to use prescription drugs than younger people, and to use over-the-counter (OTC) medications abundantly. In 1998, the elderly and the disabled accounted for 80 percent of prescription drug expenditures.[2]
- Health care costs for chronic diseases increase.

Look at Table 2.1 to appreciate how health and health care changed during the first half of the twentieth century. Note the persistence of heart disease; pharmacy's influence, specifically the discovery of antibiotics; and the appearance of mental health issues (e.g., suicide; see Chapter 8) at the end of the century.

In addition to shifting demographics, health practices and interventions throughout life influence seniors' health issues when they pass age sixty. These, too, change with time, as we learn about new prevention methods and clarify the etiology of diseases that plague people at various life stages. Careful observation and recent research have helped us understand what to expect during each stage of life and how some of these problems will affect us later.

BEFORE AGE TWENTY

Pediatric health challenges are familiar to all of us—after all, we lived through them ourselves or coped with them in our children. Otitis media, chicken pox, measles . . . We may forget some details, but generally, they are pretty straightforward. Or are they? When you think of pediatric diseases, do you include smoking? Every day, 3,000 children become smokers, and almost one-third of them will eventually lose their lives to a smoking-related disease.[3] Other children will be exposed to secondhand smoke and suffer long-term consequences (see Exhibit 2.1). And what about *Helicobacter pylori?* Most *H. pylori* infections are acquired during childhood and can wreak havoc later in life.[4]

And eating disorders? These pervasive and devastating illnesses begin in our very early years, ultimately causing dental problems and malnutrition. Other diseases of old age are now being considered pediatric diseases with geriatric outcomes, such as osteoporosis and

TABLE 2.1. Then and Now: Leading Causes of Death (in Rank Order by Incidence)

1900	1910	1920	1930	1940	1950	1998
Pneumonia*	Diseases of the heart	Pneumonia	Diseases of the heart	Diseases of the heart	Diseases of the heart	Diseases of the heart
Tuberculosis*	Pneumonia	Diseases of the heart	Pneumonia	Cancer and other malignant tumors	Malignant neoplasms	Malignant neoplasms
Diseases of the heart**	Tuberculosis	Tuberculosis	Nephritis	Intracranial lesions of vascular origin	Vascular lesions affecting the central nervous system	Cerebrovascular disease
Diarrhea, enteritis, and ulceration of the intestines*	Diarrhea, enteritis, and ulceration of the intestines	Intracranial lesions of vascular origin	Cancer and other malignant tumors	Nephritis	Accidents	Chronic obstructive pulmonary disease
Intracranial lesions of vascular origin	Intracranial lesions of vascular origin	Nephritis	Intracranial lesions of vascular origin	Pneumonia	Certain diseases of early infancy	Accidents and injuries
Nephritis*	Nephritis	Cancer and other malignant tumors	Tuberculosis	Accidents (excluding motor vehicle)	Influenza and pneumonia*	Influenza and pneumonia
Accidents (excluding motor vehicle)	Accidents (excluding motor vehicle)	Accidents (excluding motor vehicle)	Accidents (excluding motor vehicle)	Tuberculosis	Tuberculosis	Diabetes
Cancer and other malignant tumors	Cancer and other malignant tumors	Diarrhea, enteritis, and ulceration of the intestines	Premature birth	Diabetes mellitus	General ateriosclerosis	Suicide***
Senility	Premature birth	Premature birth	Motor vehicle accidents	Motor vehicle accidents	Chronic and unspecified nephritis and nephrosis	Nephritis, nephrotic syndrome, and nephrosis
Bronchitis*	Senility	Peurpural causes	Diarrhea, enteritis, and ulceration of the intestines	Premature birth	Diabetes mellitus	Chronic liver disease and cirrhosis

Source: Center for Disease Control's Leading Causes of Death, 1900-1998. Available at www.cdc.gov/nchs/data/statab/lead1900_98.pdf.
*infectious illness
**heart disease
***mental illness

13

EXHIBIT 2.1.
Cutting Edge: **Secondhand Smoke—**
An End to the Controversy?

Just how much does secondhand smoke affect children or the smoker's friends and relatives? Nicotine, the main drug in tobacco smoke, is processed by body into cotinine. TobacAlert determines the degree of tobacco smoke exposure by measuring cotinine in urine. For a nonuser of tobacco products, a positive result (1 or higher) indicates exposure to secondhand smoke in the past two to three days. It can also indicate use of cigarettes, cigars, chewing tobacco, etc., or nicotine replacement medications, such as a patch, nicotine gum, or nicotine lozenge. Usually, only tobacco or nicotine users score 3 or higher.

Quite sensitive, the test has raised awareness about secondhand smoke. Banishing a smoker to the back porch, for example, will not eliminate secondhand smoke exposure for other residents of the house. Nonsmokers exposed to residual smoke in their clothes will test positive for cotinine, often at ratings just slightly lower than those for smokers.[a]

Encouraging smokers of any age to use this test will help them understand the repercussions of tobacco use for others.

[a]Goldstein A. New home test boosts case against smoking: Detector measures passive exposure. *Washington Post.* January 19, 2004: B1.

atherosclerosis; they have their roots in childhood, but manifest in senescence.

Pharmacists should be on the lookout and ready with prevention techniques, and with interventions when prevention fails.

THE TWENTIES AND THIRTIES

Emphases in early adulthood are on sexual health, pregnancy, and establishing good health habits (e.g., dental, skin, nutrition). For women, urinary tract infections may be a nuisance with a bimodal distribution, as women in their sixties often experience a resurgence of this problem.[5] It is during their twenties and thirties that people are more prone to annoying headaches. Note, however, that although most other medical complaints tend to increase with age, the incidence of primary headache actually declines with age.[6,7]

Upper respiratory infections can be a nuisance. Toward the end of one's thirties, weight gain can be troublesome. In fact, weight gain and obesity are increasingly serious problems of youth as well.

THE FORTIES

This might be the time when nature signals the start of real aging; the onset of presbyopia (from the Greek word *presbus,* meaning "old man") may be the most troublesome clue. People notice this in various ways: for example, they may need more light when reading or working on fine tasks, or find themselves holding reading materials at arm's length to puzzle out the words on the page. Presbyopia occurs as the soft and flexible lens, which in youth readily changes shape, hardens gradually. Consequently, its focusing acuity decreases steadily. Street signs and storefronts at a distance stay clear, but telephone books and menus written in italic fonts blur frustratingly.[8]

In this decade, several other problems must be monitored, lest their persistence cause trouble later: fecal occult blood, breasts, blood pressure, and cholesterol. Weight gain can be a problem, and maintaining or even starting an exercise program is important (see Chapter 4). It is in their forties that women at risk for osteoporosis should have a baseline bone density test performed. Increasingly, osteoporosis is becoming a problem for men, and those with risk factors (hypogonadism, treatment with androgen deprivation therapy, glucocorticoid excess, alcoholism, tobacco use, thyroid and parathyroid disorders, osteomalacia, cancer, or strong family history of cancer) should also be monitored.[9]

THE FIFTIES

For women, menopause (menstruation cessation that is sustained for twelve consecutive months) generally occurs around age fifty-one, but it can happen anytime between the ages of forty and fifty-five. Smokers may experience menopause at an earlier age than the average.

The eyes can again cause difficulties late in this decade of life, with cataracts starting to form. Common symptoms include colors looking dull and brownish, difficulty differentiating among shades of blue and green, blurred vision, frequent corrective lens changes, glare and haloes, poor night vision, and difficulty finding a level of light that is just right for a given task. When such degenerative eye condition occurs, the lens gradually becomes opaque, and vision becomes misty. Although cataracts can occur as a result of other eye diseases, they primarily develop due to age. In fact, experts think that everyone would have a cataract if they lived long enough.[8]

Less common causes of cataracts include heredity, associated birth defects, chronic diseases such as diabetes, exposure to chemotherapy, and eye injury. The following medications may induce cataracts:

- Allopurinol
- Amiodarone
- Busulfan
- Clomifene
- Deferoxamine
- Glucocorticoids
- Phenothiazine derivatives
- Phenytoin
- Retinoids
- Tacrolimus
- Tamoxifene
- Tricyclics[10]

When providing pharmaceutical products for people aged fifty or older, pharmacists must keep in mind the potential for visual degradation. Remember that 5 percent of people aged sixty-five to seventy-four cannot read newsprint, and the problem worsens with age. Sixteen percent of people aged seventy-five to eighty-four cannot read newsprint, and 27 percent of those eighty-five and older cannot. Is the type on the labels you prepare as big as newsprint? Label print is a particular problem for soon-to-be seniors.[11]

THE SIXTIES AND BEYOND

As people enter their sixties, the degree to which they experience health changes depends on several factors, including family and personal health histories; dietary, exercise, and sleep habits; prescription medication use; environmental stressors; and drinking and smoking habits.[12] Some muscle and bone loss is inevitable; osteoarthritis disables about 10 percent of people who are older than sixty years, and compromises quality of life of more than 20 million Americans. Its incidence rises precipitously with age.[13] Although the weight gain that was common in the forties and fifties slows, some people find themselves shrinking in height. And, for efficient visual function, a sixty-five-year-old needs three times as much light as a twenty-year-old does.[14]

Lung Function

As we age, breathing changes in various ways. The windpipe, or trachea, and large airways increase in diameter. Alveolar enlargement reduces lung surface. A slight stiffening of the lungs expands the chest and lowers the diaphragm. By one's late sixties, the ends of the ribs may calcify to the breastbone, decreasing chest flexibility and increasing respiratory muscle strain. Coping with influenza viruses and the congestion, coughs, and wheezing caused by the flu becomes more challenging for seniors.

Blood Pressure

As we age, exercise-induced heart-rate and blood-pressure increases return to resting levels more slowly. The incidence and prevalence of hypertension seems to increase with age in industrialized societies, with a disproportionately greater increase among aging blacks than among aging whites.[15] Several studies indicate that individuals who live in isolated, low-technology societies do not experience the age-associated rise in blood pressure to the extent that people who live in industrialized nations do.[16,17]

Kidney Function

After age sixty-five, kidney mass tends to decrease, although the change is highly individual. It is unclear whether kidney function declines steadily. Age-related changes are tracked using creatinine clearance, and many pharmacists rely on the Cockcroft and Groft (C&G) formula. A mainstay for estimating renal function, C&G has certain shortcomings with respect to use in elders. For starters, it measures clearance of serum creatinine (SCr), which can be affected by weight, age, sex, muscle mass, tubular secretion, ethnicity, and diet. SCr is not a precise measurement variable. Its developers originally used twenty-four-hour urine collection creatinine clearance (ClCr) as a comparator; today, we do not bother to inconvenience patients with this collection. Also, recent studies have demonstrated that C&G underestimates ClCr in patients with a high glomerular filtration rate (GFR),[18,19,20,21] but may overestimate GFR in severely renally impaired patients.[18] Using the age factor may disadvantage C&G, because several studies suggest that old age does not significantly alter GFR,[21,22] at least in healthy older people. C&G ignores other disease states that may affect SCr or GFR, such as diabetes or cancer.[20,22,23] The following list notes drugs that depend on renal function for elimination:

Acetazolamide
Acyclovir
Allopurinol
Amantadine
Amiloride
Aminoglycosides
Atenolol
Bleomycin
Bretylium
Cephalosporins
Chlorpropamide
Cimetadine
Cisplatin
Clonidine
Diflunisal
Digoxin
Enalapril
Ethambutol
Flucytosine
Furosemide
Gold sodium thiomalate
Lithium
Methenamine
Metoclopramide
Mithromycin
Nadolol
Nitrosoureas
Penicillamine

Pentamadine   Ranitidine
Phenazopyridine   Spironolactone
Probenecid   Thiazides
Procainamide   Ticarcillin
Pyridostigmine   Vancomycin

Bladder Function

Bladder function often changes as people pass the age of sixty. Seniors, especially frail seniors, often experience asymptomatic bacteriuria (a urine culture containing less than 105 colony-forming units/mL, but with no associated symptoms).[24] Overactive bladder (OAB) is also common, with conservative estimates indicating that about 17 million people are affected, about 85 percent of them women. That rate exceeds the incidence of dementia. More liberal estimates indicate that 30 million people are affected by OAB worldwide. Most of these people are community-dwelling elders.[25] OAB symptoms fluctuate over time and may disappear spontaneously. The majority of people with incontinence can be helped, usually with a combination of behavioral interventions and medication.

Intestines

Colonic diverticula (protrusions of the mucosa through the outer muscular layers, which are usually abnormally thickened, to form narrow-necked pouches) increase with age. Diverticula can be an incidental and asymptomatic finding, a symptomatic uncomplicated disease, or a sign of diverticulitis. Many experts believe colonic diverticula are linked to low dietary fiber intake.[26,27] Adult Africans living in Africa eat a high-fiber diet; they are generally free from diverticulosis, and have stronger, wider and thinner colons than, for example, Scottish adults of the same age.[27] In Western countries, diverticular disease predominantly affects the left colon, and its prevalence increases with age. Right-sided diverticular disease is more commonly seen in Asian populations and affects younger patients.[26] Colon cancer risk also rises with age.

Thyroid Gland

The thyroid gland manufactures and secretes thyroid hormones, which influence a wide variety of body processes. The chance of having an enlarged thyroid gland increases with age. In fact, in women in their sixties, thyroid disorders become more frequent. Physicians should check thyroid function annually after age sixty.

Sleep

Aging people experience changes in their sleep patterns. The changes may be a result of normal physiologic changes associated with aging or of chronic medical conditions. Regardless, up to one-third of people older than sixty-five report symptoms of insomnia, and up to one-sixth never feel rested after waking in the morning. Up to two-thirds of patients in nursing homes have some kind of sleep disturbance.[28]

A number of nonpharmacologic interventions are available to treat insomnia, including sleep hygiene education, relaxation techniques, and sleep restriction[29,30] (see Exhibit 2.2). Should these be insufficient, the ideal hypnotic agent would have certain characteristics:

- Rapid onset (within twenty minutes)
- Duration of action long enough to maintain sleep for the entire night, but short enough to avoid residual daytime sedation
- No adverse effects
- No abuse or tolerance potential[31,32]

Dental Health

Dental health is a special concern in seniors. Tooth loss, long believed to be an inevitable consequence of aging, is no longer considered preordained. Teeth, when cared for properly, can last a lifetime. The U.S. Surgeon General's "Healthy People 2010" initiative includes several goals to improve dental care and, in particular, to reduce the rate of toothlessness among elders.[33] The oldest among our citizens have more problems in their oral cavities than our youth, who have reaped the benefits of fluorinated water and toothpaste and better oral-care education.

EXHIBIT 2.2.
Communication: Over-the-Counter Hypnotics and the Elderly

Mrs. Solaria, a frail woman in her seventies, comes to the pharmacy register with two popular OTC sleep aids that contain simple analgesics (aspirin or acetaminophen). One contains diphenhydramine, the other doxylamine succinate. She asks, "Which of these would be better for me?" You know that both first-generation antihistamines may act on muscarinic receptors to cause sedation.[a] Unfortunately, neither is ideal for the older adult. In the short term, they do decrease sleep latency and increase sleep depth and quality. When used for a short-term problem, their effectiveness is less than that of the most widely used prescription options, but better than of placebo.[b,c,d]

Good: Start by gathering information, saying, "Can you describe how often you lose sleep and why?" She says that she experiences nighttime pain and sleeplessness, losing several hours of sleep two or three nights a week. Ask, "Are you taking any pain medication during the day?" She says she takes Tylenol three times a day.

Better: In addition to your information-gathering questions, ask her whether she has fallen in the past few years, and tell her you want to pull her profile and see whether she has any condition for which these drugs might be contraindicated, such as cardiovascular disease, glaucoma, difficulty urinating, or respiratory problems. You are assessing her cognitive capability as you talk with her, and she does not appear to have dementia.

Best: Based on your knowledge of the Beers criteria, her history of a fall, and her self-reported intake of about 1,950 mg of acetaminophen every day, you cannot recommend an OTC hypnotic/analgesic for this patient.[e] You say, "Mrs. Solaria, people aged sixty-five years or older should probably avoid these medicines. And since you take pain medication during the day, this nighttime dose will put you over the limit. There are some prescription drugs for sleep that seem safer. Would you like me to call your physician?"

When she agrees, you will be prepared to discuss the issue with her physician, noting in the conversation that confusion and sedation secondary to diphenhydramine are common. A recent study of diphenhydramine use in hospitalized patients aged seventy years and older associated the drug with cognitive decline, behavioral disturbance, and increased incidence of bladder catheterization.[e,f] Residual daytime sedation and performance impairment have been associated with diphenhydramine and doxylamine. Driving, operating machinery, or undertaking other similar activities during the following day may be troublesome.[a] The actions of alcoholic beverages and

(continued)

(continued)

other medications with sedative properties are additive.[a] Recommend to the physician that they address her uncontrolled pain at her next visit, and perhaps take a prescription for a new-generation hypnotic for short-term use.

[a]Crismon ML, Canales PL. Insomnia. In Berardi RR, DeSimone EM, Newton GD, et al. (eds.), *Handbook of Nonprescription Drugs. An Interactive Approach to Self-Care,* 14th Ed. Washington, DC: American Pharmacists Association; 2004:1117-1131.

[b]Gillin JC, Byerley WF. Drug therapy: The diagnosis and management of insomnia. *N Engl J Med.* 1990;322:239-248.

[c]McEvoy GK, ed. AHFS Drug Information 2003. Bethesda, MD: American Society of Health-System Pharmacists; 2003.

[d]Rickels K, Ginsberg J, Morris RJ, et al. Doxylamine succinate in insomniac family practice patients: A double-blind study. *Curr Ther Res.* 1984;35:532-540.

[e]Fick DM, Cooper JW, Wade WE, et al. Updating the Beers criteria for potentially inappropriate medication use in older adults. *Arch Intern Med.* 2003;163:2091-2097.

[f]Agostini JV, Leo-Summers LS, Inouye SK. Cognitive and other adverse effects of diphenhydramine use in hospitalized older patients. *Arch Intern Med.* 2001;161:2091-2097.

Seniors and clinicians may have different perceptions of good oral care. Two studies that examined seniors' assessment of their own dental health found that participants often rated their dental health as good, but oral exams revealed poor conditions.[34] Early dental demise is often painless and symptomless. And elders frequently visit a dentist only when pain becomes unbearable. The problem is serious: by age fifty, 11 percent are edentulous, 42 percent have untreated dental caries extending to the root, 40 percent have gingivitis, and 70 percent have periodontitis. All of these conditions are preventable.[33] Dental disease can

- interfere with the process and pleasure of eating;
- contribute to or cause malnutrition or dehydration;
- exacerbate or create swallowing disorders;
- cause choking;
- produce bad breath;
- erode confidence or self-esteem; and

- contribute to speech problems.

Risk factors for poor oral health include poor hygiene, alcohol and tobacco use, and heredity. Mental illness and poor manual dexterity secondary to musculoskeletal conditions also contribute to poor oral health.[35] Many medications cause dry mouth, and pharmacists should remind patients who experience dry mouth to take extra time with their teeth.[36,37] Recent studies have linked poor oral health to a 2.6-fold increase in the risk of stroke,[37] and to increased risk of atherosclerosis and thrombosis.[38,39,40] The risk of respiratory infection also increases.[41,42,43]

CONCLUSION

Aging is different in each individual, and the rate of change in organ system function varies markedly among and within individuals. Age-related changes in one system are not always accompanied by changes in other systems, although sometimes organ failure can start a cascade of problems.

Normal aging and disease often manifest in the same ways. Autopsies reveal at least a few plaques and tangles in almost all ninety-year-old brains, even if the patient did not have Alzheimer's disease. Many elders have bacteriuria, often without signs or symptoms of urinary tract infection.

The rate of physiologic decline is not an unmodifiable destiny. Diet, exercise, lifestyle choices, and good preventive care can allow a sixty-year-old to have the functional capacity of a much younger person. Tobacco use, stress, and sedentary lifestyles can catapult people into premature aging.

The normal changes of aging generally do not cause suffering and death; disease processes do. Normal age-related changes reduce reserve capacity, opening the door for injuries or infections that were innocuous in youth to cause disability and dependency. Acute illness can perpetuate a downward spiral of rapid declines in health and function.

A diminished ability to maintain homeostasis and regulate body systems is a hallmark of old age. Poor compensatory mechanisms make the elderly more vulnerable to hypothermia or hyperthermia.

NOTES

1. Zemke R, Raines C, Filipczak B. *Generations at Work: Managing the Clash of Veterans, Boomers, Xers, and Nexters in Your Workplace.* New York: American Management Association; 2000.

2. Rogowski J, Lillard LA, Kington R. The financial burden of prescription drug use among elderly persons. *The Gerontologist* 1997;37:475-482.

3. Campaign for Tobacco Free Kids. Available at http://www.tobaccofreekids. org/savinglives/. Accessed December 15, 2004.

4. Wallis-Crespo MC, Crespo A. Helicobacter pylori infection in pediatric population: Epidemiology, pathophysiology, and therapy. *Fetal Pediat Pathol.* 2004; 23:11-28.

5. Hu KK, Boyko EJ, Scholes D, et al. Risk factors for urinary tract infections in postmenopausal women. *Arch Intern Med.* 2004;164:989-993.

6. Biondi DM, Saper JR. Geriatric headache. How to make the diagnosis and manage the pain. *Geriatrics* 2000;55:40-50.

7. Evans RW. Headache case studies for the primary care physician. *Med Clin North Am.* 2003;87:589-607.

8. Bron AJ, Vrensen GF, Koretz J, Maraini G, Harding JJ. The ageing lens. *Ophthalmologica* 2000;214:86-104.

9. Gilbert SM, McKiernan JM. Epidemiology of male osteoporosis and prostate cancer. *Curr Opin Urol.* 2005;15:23-27.

10. LaTour JF (ed.). Cataractes d'origine médicamenteuse. Min Dossier du CHNIM. Available at http://www.cnhim.org/b_md021.htm. Accessed January 19, 2004.

11. American Foundation for the Blind. The human eye, its functions, and visual impairment. Available at http://www.afb.org/Section.asp?DocumentID=201. Accessed December 1, 2004.

12. Resnick NM, Marcantonio ER. How should clinical care of the aged differ? *Lancet* 1997;350:1157-1158.

13. Buckwalter JA, Saltzman C, Brown T, Schurman DJ. The impact of osteoarthritis: Implications for research. *Clin Orthop.* 2004;(427 Suppl.):S6-15.

14. Kline DW, Kline TJ, Fozard JL, Kosnik W, Schieber F, Sekuler R. Vision, aging, and driving: The problems of older drivers. *J Gerontol.* 1992;47:P27-34.

15. Zemel MB, Sowers JR. Salt sensitivity and systemic hypertension in the elderly. *Am J Cardiol.* 1988;61:7H-12H.

16. Wiecek A, Kokot F. Does industrial environment influence the prevalence of arterial hypertension, plasma cholesterol and uric acid concentration and activity of the renin-aldosterone system? *Przegl Lek.* 1996;53:356-359.

17. Kokot F, Kuska J, Baczynski R, et al. Epidemiology and diagnosis of hypertension in the Upper-Silesian industrial region. IV. Serum uric acid level in normotensive and hypertensive persons in the industrialized and non-industrialized regions. *Przegl Lek.* 1982;39:535-539.

18. Lamb EJ, Webb MC, Simpson DE, et al. Estimation of glomerular filtration rate in older patients with chronic renal insufficiency: Is the modification of diet in renal disease formula an improvement? *JAGS* 2003;51:1012-1017.

19. Poole SG, Dooley MJ, Rischin D. A comparison of bedside renal function estimates and measured glomerular filtration rate (Tc^99m DTPA clearance) in cancer patients. *Ann Oncol.* 2002;13:949-955.

20. Perlemoine C, Rigalleau V, Baillet L, et al. Cockcroft's formula underestimates glomerular filtration rate in diabetic subjects treated by lipid-lowering drugs. *Diabetes Care* 2002;11:2106-2107.

21. Van Den Noortgate NJ, Janssens WH, Delanghe JR, et al. Serum cystatin C concentration compared with other markers of glomerular filtration in the old. *JAGS* 2002;50:1278-1282.

22. Burkhardt H, Bojarsky G, Gretz N, et al. Creatinine clearance, Cockcroft-Gault formula and cystatin C: Estimators of true glomerular filtration rate in the elderly? *Gerontology* 2002;48:140-146.

23. Martin L, Chatelut E, Boneu A, et al. Improvement of the Cockcroft-Gault equation for prediction of glomerular filtration in cancer patients. *Bull Cancer* 1998; 85(7):631-636.

24. Nicolle LE. Asymptomatic bacteriuria: When to screen and when to treat. *Infect Dis Clin North Am.* 2003;17:367-394.

25. Howser J. Gotta go? Study may uncover relief for overactive bladders. *Vanderbilt Medical News.* November 3, 2003. Available at http://www.mc .vanderbilt.edu/reporter/index.html?ID=2970&keywords=Surgery&start=1&end= 10. Accessed March 1, 2004.

26. Kang JY, Melville D, Maxwell JD. Epidemiology and management of diverticular disease of the colon. *Drugs Aging* 2004;21:211-228.

27. Eastwood M. Colonic diverticula. *Proc Nutr Soc.* 2003;62:31-36.

28. National Institutes of Health. Statement: The treatment of sleep disorders of older people. Consensus Development Conference, Bethesda, MD. March 26-28, 1990. *Sleep* 1991;14:169-177.

29. Morin CM, Hauri PJ, Espie CA, et al. Nonpharmacologic treatment of chronic insomnia: An American Academy of Sleep Review. *Sleep* 1999;22:1134-1156.

30. Chesson AL, Anderson WM, Littner M, et al. Practice parameters for the nonpharmacologic treatment of chronic insomnia: An American Academy of Sleep Medicine Report. *Sleep* 1999;22:1128-1133.

31. Wagner J, Wagner ML, Hening WA. Beyond benzodiazepines: Alternative pharmacologic agents for the treatment of insomnia. *Ann Pharmacother.* 1998; 32:680-691.

32. Dopheide JA, Stimmel GL. Sleep disorders. In: Koda-Kimble MA, Young LY, Kradjan WA et al. (eds.). *Applied Therapeutics: The Clinical Use of Drugs.* Philadelphia, PA: Lippincott Williams & Wilkins; 2001:Chap. 75.

33. Department of Health and Human Services. Oral health in America: A report of the Surgeon General. Available at http://www.surgeongeneral.gov/ibrary/oral health. Accessed November 17, 2001.

34. Cirincione UK, Fattore L. Improving the oral health of older adults. *Issues in Family and Community Health* 1996;18:9-30.

35. Perlman SP, Miller C. Customized oral health program. *The Exceptional Parent* 1999;29:119-124.

36. Smith RW, Columbia School of Dental and Oral Surgery staff. *Guide to Family Dental Care.* New York: W.W. Norton and Company;1997.

37. Slavkin HC, Baum BJ. Relationship of dental and oral pathology to systemic illness. *JAMA* 2000;284:1215-1217.

38. Mattila KJ, Valtonen VV, Nieminen MS, Asikainen S. Role of infection as a risk factor for atherosclerosis, myocardial infarction, and stroke. *Clin Infect Dis.* 1998;26:719-734.

39. Valtonen VV. Role of infections in atherosclerosis. *Am Heart J.* 1999;138(5 Pt 2):S431-433.

40. Epstein SE, Zhou YF, Zhu J. Infection and atherosclerosis: Emerging mechanistic paradigms. *Circulation* 1999;100:E20-28.

41. Fourrier F, Duvivier B, Boutigny H, Roussel-Delvallez M, Chopin C. Colonization of dental plaque: A source of nosocomial infections in intensive care unit patients. *Crit Care Med.* 1998;26:301-308.

42. Meurman JH, Pajukoski H, Snellman S, Zeiler S, Sulkava R. Oral infections in home-living elderly patients admitted to an acute geriatric ward. *J Dent Res.* 1997;76:1271-1276.

43. Scannapieco FA. Role of oral bacteria in respiratory infection. *J Periodontol* 1999;70:793-802.

Chapter 3

Say What? Communicating with Elders

A strange noise in the dead of the night woke elderly Mrs. Willard. When she looked out of her bedroom window and saw two men breaking into her garden shed, she telephoned the police.

"There's nobody available right now," said the sergeant, "but when someone becomes free I'll send them along to your address."

Two minutes later, she called the police again.

"I'm sorry to bother you again," she said, "but I called a couple of minutes ago about a burglary. Don't bother to send anyone—I've just shot them."

Five minutes later, police vehicles converged at both ends of the surrounding streets, and a helicopter hovered overhead with searchlights beaming. They apprehended the two burglars red-handed.

"I thought you said you'd shot them," said the police sergeant.

Mrs. Willard replied, "And I thought you said you had nobody available."

When Mrs. Willard's first communication did not work, she used what is referred to in a workplace as a "workaround": an alternative process to get the job done. For most pharmacists, communicating with seniors is a necessity, and a growing necessity at that. Poor communication based on stereotypes or misunderstandings can leave any group feeling disenfranchised and discouraged. Unfortunately, most seniors will not work around communication frustrations; they will abandon all efforts to retrieve more information and make decisions based on existing, and possibly limited or incorrect, information.

Pharmacy Practice in an Aging Society
© 2006 by The Haworth Press, Inc. All rights reserved.
doi:10.1300/5404_03

Good communication is simply a matter of common sense and good manners. It is normal to adjust our language and behavior to fit the needs of our audience. However, people who provide care or service to seniors, but who do not have a long or personal relationship with the senior, are more likely to make inappropriate, stereotype-based changes to their communication style.[1] (The worst example of this, "elderspeak," is addressed later in this chapter.)

COMMUNICATING VERBALLY
WITH THE AVERAGE SENIOR

By virtue of having lived longer than others in society, seniors represent the most heterogeneous of all age groups. They have more experience, are more able to detect insincerity or flattery, and are savvy consumers.[2] No one communication strategy will work with all seniors, but most researchers believe that face-to-face information transfer is better than written information transfer.[3] (Good communication strategies, of course, will benefit everyone, regardless of age.)

Good communication starts with good listening. Good listening has four parts:

1. Observing the speaker's verbal and nonverbal messages;
2. Interpreting the speaker's words, gestures, and behaviors, and moderating your own accordingly;
3. Allowing time for the speaker to finish expressing his or her thoughts; and
4. Providing a suitable response.

Many of us believe we are good listeners, but we often spend time thinking about what we just heard, or what we will say next, rather than really listening. Sometimes we fidget or daydream. It is important to be patient and allow time for the conversation to flow, especially when communicating with elders. People generally respond to care better and live longer when they are socially engaged and communicate with others daily. Pharmacists can improve communication without necessarily increasing the amount of time it takes.[4]

SETTING THE STAGE

Seniors have different values than younger people; remember that they are conservative, unlikely to take risks, respect authority, and expect respect.[5] You will need to begin to establish your credibility early by introducing yourself and explaining who you are, and offering to shake hands, if doing so is culturally appropriate. These actions begin to establish credibility because they indicate you are well-mannered and educated. You will further enhance your credibility by employing good nonverbal skills, as described later. Start the conversation with why you want to talk. Some seniors will prefer that you talk with their trusted relative or friend (called a "key informant" by information specialists). Be sure, however, that the senior gives permission before you talk with anyone else about his or her personal matters.

Elders may not be able to easily block or ignore background noise, like television or background music; noise can cause inattentiveness.[2] Therefore, before beginning the discussion, take steps to minimize background noise of any kind and establish an environment that is conducive to conversation. Also, if possible, remove physical barriers, such as desks, and offer comfortable seating.

When speaking and listening, maintain eye contact, glancing away from time to time so you do not appear to be staring or glaring. (A discussion of culture goes beyond the scope of this chapter, but if your clientele is culturally diverse, you will need to brush up on culturally sensitive communication.) Touch the patient lightly on the hand or arm, if the patient appears comfortable with this kind of contact. Do not touch patients who look uncomfortable or guard their personal space by pulling away or withdrawing. Avoid copious note-taking and looking at the clock. If you are telling a patient how to do something, tell him verbally and then show him. Finally, ask him to repeat the advice and/or demonstrate the process. The following list offers advice on how to counsel an elder:

- Provide paper and pencil, and ask the patient to take a few minutes and jot down any questions or topics of concern.
- Unless they tell you otherwise, assume patients want to be called "Mr. X" or "Mrs. Y."

- Most people prefer to say "yes," and seem agreeable. Use open-ended questions (questions that cannot be answered "yes" or "no") to elicit information.
- Summarize what the patient has said, so he or she can verify that you understood them.
- Avoid professional jargon. Use words the patient will understand (some people call this "living room language"). Listening carefully to the patient will help you determine how sophisticated your explanation can be. That is, talk to the person, not the hair color.
- Gently reinforce or repeat key points. Summarizing at the end is a good way to repeat key points inoffensively.
- Use a familiar framework to explain points. A retired mechanic with liver disease will appreciate an analogy that compares his liver to a filter. A retired secretary will appreciate having her husband's memory problems described as a filing system error.
- Offer written materials to back up what you tell the patient.
- If it seems like the patient does not understand what you are saying, rephrase rather than repeat the information. Use different words and simpler sentence structure.
- Ask the patient to summarize what he or she has learned. Say "Show me," "Tell me in your own words," or "Teach me back." Gently guide the patient if he or she has forgotten or is confused.

Avoid engaging patients in parallel cognitive tasks; for example, do not point to a picture on the correct use of a nebulizer while explaining medication effects at the same time. Instead, explain one step verbally (maintaining eye contact), then point to the picture. Proceed to the next step.

Seniors expect you to do what you say you will do. They consider your words a promise.[5] If you say you will find additional information and mail it to them, or that you will call with more facts tomorrow, follow through.

COMMUNICATING IN WRITING

Reminders are helpful for everyone, not just seniors; therefore, providing written backup materials is important. Written materials will be more effective if they consider general trends observed in aging populations and accommodate changes of later life. For example, seniors have more difficulty reading text containing words of varying font sizes than younger people do.[6] Using twelve-point fonts or larger is best. Avoid using all upper-case letters. They are harder for people with poor literacy skills to read, and imply a scolding tone. Including or drawing pictures may enhance understanding and the ability to recall the information later. The following list gives additional tips on written materials:

- Keep text at eighth- to ninth-grade reading level; most word processing packages now calculate reading levels.[7,8]
- Repeat important messages using callouts or summaries.
- Assemble an advisory committee of seniors in your area to test-read materials.[2]
- Use specific examples to illustrate general ideas. Instead of saying, "Take an analgesic," say, "Take a pain reliever, like aspirin or ibuprofen."
- Write in short, positive sentences instead of complicated or negative sentences. "Do not store this medication in a humid area" becomes "Store your medicine in a cool, dry place."
- Use active voice. "The prescription was taken to the pharmacy by your sister" becomes "Your sister took the prescription to the pharmacy."
- Use visuals that relate to the topic you are describing.
- Punctuate appropriately and use italics only sparingly, as italics are the hardest fonts to read. Small print and pictures without captions impede reading, too.[9]
- Keep paragraphs short.
- Insert simple, catchy headings.
- Use plenty of white space as well as bright colors that provide clear contrast.

About 95 percent of individuals aged fifty-five and older need glasses to improve vision.[10,11] Among those older than eighty-five, 55 percent report that glasses only partially correct visual problems, and 12 percent are legally blind.[11,12] The consequences of vision loss range from inconvenient to dangerous. Use the following tips to communicate effectively with seniors who are visually impaired:

- Know the signs that someone is visually impaired, but possibly in denial. They bump into objects; move hesitantly or walk close to the wall; grope or touch things uncertainly; squint or tilt the head to see; ask for different lighting; hold reading material close to or far from the face; drop food or utensils at mealtimes; seem to have difficulty making out faces or room and floor numbers; are confused or disoriented in familiar environments.
- Ask people whether they are having trouble seeing or need their glasses or a magnifier.
- Recognize that people with age-related macular degeneration may need to be reminded to move objects to their peripheral vision and look at them from the corner of the eye.
- Be familiar with low-vision aids that magnify print on curved surfaces; these will help the visually impaired read prescription bottles.
- Enlarge images when possible, using a photocopier's "enlarge" function. Increase the size of your font, if possible.
- Purchase large-button telephones and calculators and suitable clocks if your clientele need to use these items.
- Use higher-wattage and higher-intensity light sources directed toward the task (as opposed to the person).
- Remove or secure rugs, low tables, and clutter, and install railings on stairs or porches.
- Employ dramatic color contrast among furnishings, avoiding a monochromatic décor. Use color contrast on prescription vials, too, tagging one drug yellow and another bright blue.
- Use texture, too, to mark things. Wrapping one rubber band around a diuretic bottle and two around a vitamin bottle will help a visually impaired person differentiate between the containers.
- Offer to help, but let the visually impaired person indicate the type of help needed.
- If the person's vision is badly impaired, announce yourself as you approach and, if the person does not know you well, indicate why you are there. A handshake is a good way to help orient the person to your presence.
- Greet the person by name (if he or she will recognize your voice), so he or she knows who is approaching. Also, let the person know when you are leaving the room.

- Avoid changing your speech pattern (e.g., talking louder) or shying away from topics for fear of embarrassing the person. Like anyone else, visually impaired people want to know whether they have spinach in their teeth.[10,11,12,13]

According to the National Center for Education Statistics, approximately 23 percent of American adults are classified as having the lowest literacy proficiency (i.e., difficulty reading more than a few words), and the likelihood of illiteracy is highest for adults over the age of sixty-five. As another 27 percent have marginal literacy skills, you can expect fully half of your clientele to have reading difficulties. The poor proficiency is probably because adults in the oldest age groups completed less formal schooling (10.7 years on average) than did younger adults (12.5 to 13.1 years on average).[14]

People with inadequate literacy skills come from a variety of backgrounds and have no visible signs of the disability. They are often verbally quite articulate. Functionally illiterate adults are more likely to have more health problems, to live in poverty, and to have fewer years of education. Literacy problems are twice as common for Americans over sixty-five years of age and among inner-city minorities.[15] However, many illiterate people are financially quite successful. Printed materials must be easy to read and well formatted, but these materials alone will not close the communication gap.

Many adults, particularly those with literacy problems, find videos of health information helpful. They can play them over, stop and rewind, and share them with key informants. A National Institutes of Health Web site for seniors, http://nihseniorhealth.gov, features larger print and an audio function that permits seniors to listen instead of read. Recent versions of Adobe Acrobat Reader offer a "Read Out Loud" function (click View and select Read Out Loud from the drop-down table). It sounds remarkably good for a computer. Most public libraries offer videos and audiotapes describing health conditions.

ELDERSPEAK

Elderspeak is patronizing speech similar to baby talk or motherese, recognizable by its slow rate, exaggerated intonation, high pitch, loud volume, repetitive content, and simple vocabulary and grammar.[4,16] The typical elderspeak user structures sentences around diminutives (honey, sweetie, big guy, young fellow), collective pronouns (we, us), and tags on phrases that eliminate choice (Won't you? Wouldn't you? Can't you?).[17,18] O'Connor and St. Pierre call it "the 'special' verbal and nonverbal behaviors otherwise reserved for infants and pets."[1]

People who use elderspeak are often reacting to stereotypes about elders' competence, autonomy, and communication skills.[1] Many elders find elderspeak offensive, perceiving that it questions their competence, implies they are more dependent or less intelligent than they are, and is not nurturing.[4,13,16] Clinicians should note that although baby talk serves a function, and the unique language that develops between lovers is indicative of trust, elderspeak does not improve comprehension.[4,16] The astute reader will see that elderspeak shares some of the principles of good communication discussed above: repeating or expanding directions, asking questions, and decreasing word and sentence complexity. These can be beneficial, but elderspeak goes overboard.[16] Exhibit 3.1 gives examples of elderspeak, and ways to improve it.

EXHIBIT 3.1.
Communication: Eliminating Elderspeak

Overly nurturing or controlling communication—"Good morning, sweetie! Are we here to pick up a refill? We can wait a few minutes, can't we?"—or addressing a clearly senior customer as, "Young fellow, I told you it would be a while. Wait here."

Improved communication: "Good morning, Mrs. Donohue. Did you call in a refill? Can you wait about ten minutes?" or "Hello, Mr. Zellmer. I'm not quite done with your refill yet."

Best communication: "Good morning, Mrs. Donohue. What can we do for you today?" (She says she called in a refill.) "Which refill did you call in? Would you like me to check if anything else needs to be refilled, too?" or "Hello, Mr. Zellmer. You're quicker than I am today, so your refill is not quite ready. Would you like to sit here for a few minutes, or browse?"

Source: Adapted from Williams K, Kemper S, Hummert ML. Enhancing communication with older adults: Overcoming elderspeak. *J Gerontol Nurs.* 2004;30:17-25.

UNIQUE COMMUNICATION ISSUES
WITH DEMENTIA

People with Alzheimer's disease and other forms of dementia often have difficulty communicating. Hallmarks of Alzheimer's disease include struggling to find the right words (and inventing new words instead; see Chapter 9) and/or forgetting the meanings of words and phrases. Reliance on gestures (such as hand gestures or pointing to objects) increases as verbal skills decline.

People with dementia can communicate in meaningful ways into the later stages of the disease. If caregivers and clinicians are patient enough to interpret the communication, patient-centered interventions are possible and may reduce troublesome behaviors.[19] An elder who develops dementia will retain his or her history and experiences; these will color the expression of his or her dementia in terms of behaviors, verbalizations, and perceptions.[20] The strategies detailed below improve communication with Alzheimer's disease and other dementia patients.

- Get the patient's attention before you begin talking. Reduce background noise from any source (music, health videos playing, babies crying, cash registers clanging). Always approach an Alzheimer's patient from the front so he or she can see you, address the patient by name, and identify yourself. Repeat the patient's name often throughout the conversation; this helps him or her focus.[21,22]
- Maintain eye contact. Monitor the patient's facial expressions and body language for anger, frustration, agitation, or lack of comprehension. Keep your own expression friendly, and keep your hands away from your face, so the patient can see your expression.
- Be attentive. Show that you are listening and trying to understand what is being said. Use pauses to give the person time to process what you are saying. Alzheimer's patients need time to concentrate, comprehend, and formulate a response, so allow up to a minute or two for response.
- Speak naturally and remain gentle and relaxed. Avoid talking too loudly, and speak at a normal rate. Use short, simple, and fa-

miliar words. If you need to raise your voice to be heard, lower the tone (pitch).

- Simple, positive language is essential. Give one-step directions using short words and sentences of no more than four words, conveying only one message or thought. Ask only one question at a time. Avoid pronouns; identify people and things by name. Instead of telling people what *not* to do, suggest what they *should* do. For example, instead of saying, "Don't go into that aisle," say, "Let's go into this counseling room."
- Rephrase rather than repeat if the patient seems to misunderstand you. Say it differently instead of saying the same thing louder.
- Adapt to your listener. Try to understand the words and gestures the patient uses to communicate. Family members may be able to help in this area because they have known the patient for years. In stressful situations, it is acceptable to use the patient's memory loss to your advantage. Distract or redirect the patient from distressing situations, and the patient may forget what was upsetting.
- Humor is a durable personality trait that often remains intact as dementia progresses.[20] Alzheimer's patients will appreciate appropriate humor. Allow (and appreciate) patients' attempts to express humor, especially in difficult and trying situations.[20]
- Encourage the person to continue to express his or her thoughts, even if he or she is having difficulty. Do not interrupt, criticize, correct, or argue. If it seems like you are not getting through, regardless of what you say and how you say it, ask the patient whether you could reschedule the discussion. Using the key informant principle to your advantage, ask whether there is someone who might talk with you first and then help make things clearer to the patient. Say, "Is there someone you trust who explains things better than me who might help us?"
- Never assume that a patient is completely oblivious. Dementia patients' abilities fluctuate. Talking about a patient to another person in front of the patient as though the latter is invisible is inconsiderate and demeaning.

COMMUNICATING WITH AGITATED PATIENTS

Clinicians who work in long-term care and psychiatric facilities are trained to recognize escalating behaviors, agitation, and negative emotion in their patients. It is not difficult to learn to do this, and once you begin to look for these signs, you will recognize them in others— customers, children, family members, etc.—and be better able to de-escalate conflict.

Generally, people express frustration, fear, hostility, and aggression by increasing body movement and agitation. They become restless. They may pace or rock from side to side. As their agitation escalates, they might kick things, rattle doorknobs, make fists, or wave their arms. A cardinal sign of agitation in the cognitively impaired or psychotic patient is pushing furniture. And, of course, anger leads to grimacing, frowning, or darting eyes; increased speech volume and higher pitch; and fight-or-flight symptoms (rapid breathing, widening of the eyes, dilating pupils, and tightening of muscle tone).[23,24]

When agitation becomes apparent, several tactics can de-escalate the situation. Your behavior should be the reverse of the agitated patient's behavior. Stay calm and reassuring; reduce environmental noise and lower your voice; disperse crowds or slowly move to a less crowded vicinity; remove dangerous objects from the area; do not pressure the patient or make additional demands; and make certain that all your communications, verbal and nonverbal, are consistent.[23,24]

Be aware also that patients who have dementia or become agitated may be reacting to a trigger—something that makes them angry or uncomfortable. If agitation assumes a pattern, look for triggers.[23,24] The trigger can be environmental, such as bright lights or noise. It can be physiological, like an undiagnosed urinary tract infection or a sore muscle. It can also be a certain staff member or person whom the patient simply dislikes.

CONCLUSION

Good manners and common sense dictate that you treat all patients with dignity and respect. This means listening carefully and deferring to the patient's communication style, abilities, and preferences. The same rules that apply to communication with anyone also apply to seniors, but with a few commonsense modifications and an understanding of underlying pathologies that may hamper discussion.

The Bum's Rush

- *Pharmacists who would like more information about communication with elders will find Health Canada's booklet* Communicating with Seniors *(available at http://dsp-psd.pwgsc.gc.ca/Collection/H88-3-26-11999E.pdf) most helpful.*
- *Pharmacists who work with minority populations should purchase a text on cultural competence.*
- *The best judges of your ability to communicate with seniors are seniors themselves. Establish a panel of seniors (invite them via your local senior centers) and ask them to survey your workplace. They will gladly tell you what works and what does not.*

NOTES

1. O'Connor BP, St Pierre ES. Older persons' perceptions of the frequency and meaning of elderspeak from family, friends, and service workers. *Int J Aging Hum Dev.* 2004;58:197-221.

2. Health Canada. Communicating with seniors. Available at http://dsp-psd.pwgsc.gc.ca/Collection/H88-3-26-1999E.pdf. Accessed November 11, 2004.

3. Harrington J, Noble LM, Newman SP. Improving patients' communication with doctors: A systematic review of intervention studies. *Patient Educ Couns.* 2004;52:7-16.

4. Williams K, Kemper S, Hummert ML. Improving nursing home communication: An intervention to reduce elderspeak. *Gerontologist* 2003;43:242-247.

5. Zemke R, Raines C, Filipczak B. *Generations at Work: Managing the Clash of Veterans, Boomers, Xers, and Nexters in Your Workplace.* New York: American Management Association; 2000.

6. Strizver I. Designing for seniors. Available at http://www.fonts.com/fonten/fontent_home.asp?nCo=AFMT&con=fyti_designing_seniors. Accessed December 1, 2004.

7. Davis TC, Wolf MS. Health literacy: Implications for family medicine. *Fam Med.* 2004;36:595-598.

8. Wallace LS, Lennon ES. American academy of family physicians patient education materials: Can patients read them? *Fam Med.* 2004;36:571-574.

9. Hoarau H, Kantor G. Understanding the information booklet "For a better understanding of radiotherapy." *Cancer Radiother.* 2000;4:308-316.

10. Medline plus. Aging changes in the senses. Available at http://www.nlm.nih .gov/medlineplus/ency/article/004013.htm. Accessed November 30, 2004.

11. National Eye Institute. Statistics and data. Available at http://www.nei.nih .gov/eyedata/. Accessed November 30, 2004.

12. Campbell VA, Crews JE, Moriarty DG, Zack MM, Blackman DK. Surveillance for sensory impairment, activity limitation, and health-related quality of life among older adults—United States, 1993-1997. *MMWR CDC Surveill Summ.* 1999;48(8):131-156.

13. Living with vision loss: A handbook for caregivers. Canadian National Institute for the Blind, 2003. Available at http://www.cnib.ca/eng/publications/ pamphlets/lwvl/index.htm#toc. Accessed November 30, 2004.

14. U.S. Department of Education. National Center for Education Statistics. Adult literacy in the United States, NCES. Available at http://nces.ed.gov/pubs93/93275 .pdf. Accessed November 30, 2004.

15. Kirsch I, Jungeblut A, Jenkins L, et al. *Adult literacy in America: A first look at the results of the National Adult Literacy Survey.* Washington, DC: National Center for Education Statistics; 1993.

16. Kemper S, Harden T. Experimentally disentangling what's beneficial about elderspeak from what's not. *Psychol Aging.* 1999;14:656-670.

17. Williams K, Kemper S, Hummert ML. Enhancing communication with olderadults: Overcoming elderspeak. *J Gerontol Nurs.* 2004;30:17-25.

18. Ryan EB, Hamilton JM, See SK. Patronizing the old: How do younger and older adults respond to baby talk in the nursing home? *Int J Aging Hum Dev.* 1994;39:21-32.

19. Acton GJ, Mayhew PA, Hopkins BA, Yauk S. Communicating with individuals with dementia. The impaired person's perspective. *J Gerontol Nurs.* 1999;25:613.

20. Buckwalter KC, Gerdner LA, Hall GR, Stolley JM, Kudart P, Ridgeway S. Shining through: The humor and individuality of persons with Alzheimer's disease. *J Gerontol Nurs.* 1995;21:11-16.

21. Hendryx-Bedalov PM. Alzheimer's dementia: Coping with communication decline. *J Gerontol Nurs.* 2000;26:20-24.

22. Tappen RM, Williams-Burgess C, Edelstein J, Touhy T, Fishman S. Communicating with individuals with Alzheimer's disease: Examination of recommended strategies. *Arch Psychiatr Nurs.* 1997;11:249-256.

23. Sherman C. Agitation, aggression demand clinical acumen: Practical psychopharmacology; What experts say to do before study results are in. *Clinical Psychiatry News* 2001;29:20.

24. Alexopoulos GS, Silver JM, Kahn DA, Frances A, Carpenter D. (eds.). *The Expert Consensus Guideline Series: Agitation in Older Persons with Dementia.* A Postgraduate Medicine Special Report. The McGraw-Hill Companies, Inc.; 1998. Available at www.psychguides.com/gagl.pdf. Accessed May 22, 2006.

Chapter 4

Exercise and Aging

Did you hear about the older lady who decided to attend an exercise class? She went to the class, jumped, stooped, bent, ran, skipped, stood on her head, and pulled. The sad part is that by the time she finally got the leotards on, the class was over.

Many Americans believe that muscle loss and weakness are irreversible consequences of aging. They also think people with chronic disorders should avoid exercise, that they need specialized equipment (other than custom-designed leotards), and that a healthy diet is more important than exercise. Incorrect on all counts! Many seniors use the first unpleasant exercise-induced sensation as an excuse to decorate the couch, thinking discomfort signals injury.[1,2] This leads to the adage, "You know you're into middle age when you realize that caution is the only thing you care to exercise." In fact, seniors (even those in their eighties and nineties) and people with chronic conditions such as arthritis and hypertension benefit more than healthy younger people from proper exercise.[3] Some benefits include the following:

- increased strength
- improved balance (fall prevention)
- improved mental health
- lower overall mortality
- decreased risk for coronary heart disease
- increased oxygen consumption
- changes in glucose metabolism, improved insulin response
- improved lipid profile, decreased cholesterol
- lower risk for diabetes

Pharmacy Practice in an Aging Society
© 2006 by The Haworth Press, Inc. All rights reserved.
doi:10.1300/5404_04

- lower risk for hypertension
- improved functioning with arthritis
- improved activities of daily living skills and quality of life[4,5]

Since 1986 we have known that death rates decrease as energy expended in exercise increases. Paffenberger et al., in a classic study, followed Harvard graduates for years.[6] Graduates who reported less exercise died earlier, with cardiovascular or respiratory causes of death leading the way. Death rates declined steadily as energy expended increased from less than 500 to 3,500 kcal per week. Expending more than 2,000 kcal by walking, playing sports, or climbing stairs weekly decreased mortality by one-quarter to one-third. After considering confounding variables, including hypertension, cigarette smoking, extremes or gains in body weight, and early parental death, mortality rates were significantly lower among the physically active.[6] Yet, health care providers discuss activity or exercise levels with fewer than half of their patients, and with even fewer older adults.[4] (For information on exercise in America, see Exhibit 4.1.)

AGING AND MUSCLE LOSS

Around age thirty, sarcopenia (age-associated muscle loss) begins, and by age eighty, unless one exercises, as much as 60 percent of muscle strength may be lost.[7] Overall, by age eighty, lean muscle mass and muscle endurance (the ability to sustain exercise) decrease by 30 to 40 percent relative to total body mass.[1] Sarcopenia can lead to ambulation problems, increased dependence, age-related disabilities resulting from falls and fractures, increased risk for muscle injuries, and prolonged recovery times.[7,8]

CLASSIC STUDIES

Fiatarone and colleagues' early study is noteworthy because of its ten participants' ages: eighty-six to ninety-six.[9] The researchers demonstrated that muscle loss among seniors is reversible. The nine subjects who completed two months of high-intensity resistance training increased leg strength by 174 percent and mid-thigh muscle mass by 9 percent. Activities of daily living (ADL) improved significantly—

EXHIBIT 4.1.
Statistics at a Glance: Exercising in America

- Only 31 percent of adults between the ages of sixty-five and seventy-four, and 23 percent of those over seventy-five engage in routine physical activity several times a week.[a]
- Up to two-thirds of older adults, women, those with low incomes, and those with less education[b] do not engage in any exercise activity.[c]
- Of sedentary adults aged fifty and over who start an exercise program, 50 percent stop within the first six months.[d]
- If 10 percent of adults engaged in a regular walking program, insurers would save at least $5.6 billion in heart-disease-related costs.[e-h]
- Groups that just stand or walk around the house for two hours daily are 9 percent less obese and have 12 percent less diabetes than sedentary groups.[e-h]
- Groups that engage in one hour of brisk walking daily are 24 percent less obese and have 34 percent less incidence of diabetes than sedentary groups.[e-h]

[a]U.S. Agency for Healthcare Research and Quality, CDC. *Physical activity and older Americans: Benefits and strategies.* Washington, DC: AHRQ; 2000. Available at http://www.ahrq.gov/ppip/activity.htmb. Accessed June 6, 2003.

[b]U.S. Department of Health and Human Services, CDC. *Physical Activity and Health: A Report of the Surgeon General.* Washington, DC: CDC; 2003. Available at http://www.cdc.gov/nccdphp/sgr/ataglan.htm. Accessed June 2003.

[c]U.S. Department of Health and Human Services, National Institute of Aging. *Exercise: A Guide from the National Institute of Aging. 2001,* NIH Publication No. 10-4258.

[d]Resnick B. A seven-step approach to starting an exercise program for older adults. *Patient Educ Couns.* 2000;39:243-252.

[e]U.S. Agency for Healthcare Research and Quality. *Preventing disability in the elderly with chronic disease. Research in Action.* 2002. AHRQ Pub 02-0018.

[f]Whitehouse K. Exercise can curb medical bills. *Wall Street Journal.* April 29, 2003.

[g]Department of Health and Human Services, CDC. *Preventing obesity and chronic diseases through good nutrition and physical activity.* Available at www.cdc.gov/nccdphp/pe_factsheets/pe_pa.htm. Accessed June 6, 2003.

[h]Hu FB, Li TY, Colditz GA, et al. Television watching and other sedentary behaviors in relation to risk of obesity and type 2 diabetes mellitus. *JAMA.* 2003;289:1785-1789.

gait speed increased by 48 percent, and two of the participants traded walkers for less restrictive canes following training. After the training period, participants once again reverted to a sedentary lifestyle and lost an average of 32 percent of muscle strength in four weeks.[9]

A later, larger study randomly assigned 100 elderly (average age of 87.1) participants to resistance weight training or to a control group that engaged in recreational and leisure activities. After ten weeks, weight training participants increased muscle strength by an average of 113 percent (3 percent for controls), gait speed by 12 percent (controls declined 1 percent), and stair-climbing agility and endurance by 28 percent (4 percent in controls). Four weight trainers swapped walkers for canes. In addition, in exercisers, thigh muscle mass increased by 3 percent, while placebo subjects' thighs decreased in mass by 2 percent. With 51 percent of participants cognitively impaired, mental capacity was not necessarily a barrier to exercise.[10]

The impact of these findings is twofold. First, weight training (not to be confused with aerobic exercise) can reverse seniors' muscle loss. Second, numerous studies link lower extremity function to functional abilities (walking speed, balance, and rising from a chair) and ADLs. One study, for example, correlated poor lower extremity function with disability four years later.[7] Another randomized, controlled study assigned 188 people aged seventy-five or older to a six-month exercise program. At three months, seven months, and twelve months, exercisers demonstrated measurably less ADL decline than controls.[11] The following section describes simple but effective exercises for seniors.

EXERCISE FOR ELDERS

Seniors don't need heavy weights or bulging muscles. Beginning weight training with three-pound weights or intact soup cans (and increasing the weights gradually to five to eight pounds) confers benefit. It also strengthens the skeleton, which lowers fracture risk.

The following exercises, performed as two slow, easy sets of eight to twelve repetitions (resting between sets) two or three times a week, can improve quality of life significantly.

- *Arms.* Sitting in a sturdy chair, hold the weights (start with the lightest ones) alongside the chair, parallel to your torso. Lift one weight at a time, bending your elbow and turning your palm toward your shoulder. Stop just before touching the shoulder, and return the weight to your side.
- *Shoulders.* Still sitting, keep your back straight and lean forward slightly with your feet flat on the ground. Again, start with the arms hanging down. Without locking your elbows, raise your arms to the sides, palms down, until the weight is at shoulder height or just above. Then lower the weight slowly back to the starting position.
- *Hips and buttocks.* Wearing ankle weights, turn the chair to face away from you. Lean slightly forward, supporting yourself by holding the chair's back. Lift one leg behind you, with your knee slightly bent. Lift the leg only as far as you can without straining. Switch legs for each repetition.
- *Legs.* Still supporting your weight by holding the back of the chair, stand up straight and bend one knee, raising the lower part of the leg as if aiming to touch your rear with your heel. Then lower the leg. Complete a full set of repetitions with one leg before working the other.
- *Thighs.* With the ankle weights on, sit on the chair and place a rolled-up towel under your knees (which should be close to the seat's edge). Extend your lower leg straight out, and then return it. Switch legs for each lift.
- *Stomach.* Lie on your back, bend your knees, and place your feet flat on the floor twelve inches apart. With your hands resting on your thighs and your chin tucked to your chest, raise your shoulders off the floor. Hold for a moment, and then lower your shoulders.[12]

METHODOLOGICAL CONSIDERATIONS

Studies looking at exercise in the elderly are becoming more frequent, but interpret study results carefully. Methodological issues are common. For example, few studies tabulate the number of potential participants who refused to participate or were excluded for other reasons. Second, many studies targeting the frail elderly operationally define frailty by age. Ideally, frailty should be defined with functional measures. Criteria for establishing frailty include

- age greater than eighty-five,
- dependence in more than one activity of daily living,
- three or more comorbid conditions, and
- one or more geriatric syndromes: incontinence, dementia, delirium, falls, neglect/abuse, osteoporosis.[13]

Researchers sometime omit descriptions of exercise interventions; they should specify each exercise's intensity, duration, weights employed, and types and numbers of repetitions. Finally, remember that studies with null or negative results often go unpublished. You can only interpret the relevance of positive findings against the total number of studies (positive and null or negative).

That said, recommend moderate exercise, but advise men over the age of forty, women over the age of fifty, people who have a family history of early-onset cardiovascular disease, and people with moderate-to-severe health problems to check with their physician first.

EXERCISE, FALLS, AND OSTEOPOROSIS

Falls remain the leading cause of injury in people over sixty-five, responsible for 95 percent of hip fractures among elders, and more fatal traumatic brain injury than one might expect. Every hour, an older person dies as the result of a fall.[14]

Proven methods to prevent falls include medication adjustment, environmental design (e.g., installing grab bars, improved lighting), prescribing calcium and vitamin D supplements, and reducing environmental hazards (e.g., deep-pile carpeting). Exercise can help, too, especially if it supplements other interventions.[15]

Osteoporosis, which affects more than 25 million Americans, leads to 250,000 hip fractures each year.[16] Approximately 80 percent of the victims of osteoporosis are women, who lose bone mass at a rate of about 1 percent a year after age thirty-five (increasing 2 percent to 3 percent a year after menopause).[16,17] For this reason, adequate calcium and vitamin D intake is essential for women.

Researchers are beginning to acknowledge that the disease is a significant problem among older men, too. Osteoporosis is especially problematic for men on androgen deprivation therapy, or institutionalized or bedridden and therefore inactive. The newest treatments for prostate cancer, which are widely used, also cause osteoporosis. Many pharmacies now offer bone mineral density screening, and pharmacists might use these occasions to discuss exercise with seniors.

Muscle strength correlates with bone mass because site-specific muscular contractions increase bone mass density.[17] Lack of physical activity is a significant risk factor for osteoporotic fractures,[16] and the risk of hip and vertebral fractures increases as bone density decreases. Exercise preserves bone, but seniors must sustain the exercise (so easy to say, so difficult to do) for it to be effective. Inactivity is also a risk factor for disabilities related to osteoarthritis of the knee and hip.

Based on inarguable evidence,[18-20] the American College of Rheumatology recommends exercise as a standard osteoarthritis treatment for at-risk elders.[18] The Mayo Clinic's slide show (available at http://www.mayoclinic.com /invoke.cfm?objectid=84CA40A5-3929-4A66-80A246E424E70329&slide=8&isagg =0&ref=39187AB8-CEFC-43C0-808D367B7CD35305) has numerous easy exercises for people at risk for or with osteoporosis. However, be cautious about recommending specific exercises until you consult with the patient's physician. Patients in the later stages of bone density decline can hurt themselves when engaging in high-impact exercise.

CARDIOVASCULAR HEALTH

The average person loses about 10 percent of his or her aerobic capacity every decade, although the loss is not linear. In addition to increasing quality of life and self-sufficiency, lifelong frequent exercise can add four to five years to life.[21] When seniors commit to exercising for four months, they improve their aerobic capacity by 1 to 4 percent. With ongoing exercise, aerobic power, body composition, oxygen consumption, and lipid profiles continue to improve, especially in men.[22-24] Maximum cardiac workload, ejection fraction, stroke volume, and cardiovascular index also improve.[25]

IMMUNE FUNCTION AND CANCER

Immunocompetence and cancer are naturally associated. Immuno-senescence seems to occur primarily in the lymphocyte components of immunocompetence cells. Over time, T cells decline, T-cell responsiveness fades, and lymphocyte subset distribution shifts. (Subsets consist of T [thymic-dependent] and B [bone marrow-derived] cells further differentiated with various surface markers; changes can influence the patient's ability to defend against infection or cancer.) Increased disease susceptibility, incidence of autoimmune disease, and cancer rates follow.[26,27]

Unfortunately, good, long-term studies examining immunocompetence and exercise in humans are limited, usually by small sample sizes. However, exercise-trained animals have improved T-cell-mediated immune function that sedentary controls lack.[28]

Cancer researchers are extremely interested in this topic, especially as it relates to prevention of tumor recurrence. Because exercise seems to ameliorate the fatigue that plagues many cancer patients, much research is underway right now.[29]

Exercise intensity and disease susceptibility can be plotted graphically (see Figure 4.1); a J-shaped curve results.[30] The exercise-immunocompetence curve is J-shaped because intense or erratic exercise taxes the immune system, causing its suppression.[26] Regular, moderate exercise in previously sedentary elderly subjects increases natural killer, neutrophil, and macrophage populations; leads to a partial resumption of T-cell responsiveness; and improves overall immune function.[26,27,31]

Exercise studies in cancer patients are of great interest for several reasons:

- In older men (average age 68.2) with androgen-deprivation-treated prostate cancer, resistance exercise improved drug-induced fatigue, reduced functional decline, increased body fat, and decreased lean body mass.[32]
- A few weeks of exercise may produce results approximately equivalent to those achieved with costly erythropoietin therapy.[32] Exercise decreases fatigue on the day of and the day after exercise, so frequent exercise works best.[29]

- Patient participation in exercise programs, even among seniors, often exceeds researchers' expectations (with attendance usually higher than 70 percent).[29,30,32]
- Exercise may effectively prevent weight gain secondary to adjuvant treatment of breast cancer.
- Exercise decreases the duration of chemotherapy-induced neutropenia, increases achievable walking distance, increases leg strength, improves natural-killer-cell cytolytic activity, and increases the proportion of circulating granulocytes.[33]

MENTAL HEALTH

Although no one knows why, exercise improves mental health even more than social contact does.[21] Exercise of any sort may improve and even prevent depression and anxiety. More active people, especially women and elders, are less likely to develop depression or anxiety. This suggests a dose-response relationship.[34] Although the evidence concerning the utility of exercise when added to psychological or psychiatric care is inconclusive,[21] the National Insti-

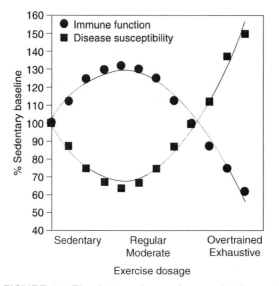

FIGURE 4.1. The J-shaped curve for exercise intensity.

tute of Mental Health considers the evidence suggestive enough to endorse exercise as a valid treatment strategy for anxiety and depression.[33,35]

Exercise also benefits sleep and memory, as shown by a small study of subjects aged sixty-five to ninety-two who engaged in low-intensity exercise and paired social interaction daily. Subjects who participated in two ninety-minute programs of light exercise daily had increased amounts of slow-wave sleep and, further, demonstrated improvement in memory-oriented tasks following the intervention.[36] Researchers propose that exercise, like light and social stimuli, is an external "zeitgeber" (i.e., a circadian synchronizing agent). Age-associated circadian rhythm changes interfere with sleep and increase daytime drowsiness. Increasing exercise redefines day and night for people in whom these cycles have been disrupted.[36,37]

Impaired or diminishing cognitive ability should not put a stop to exercise. Many dementia sufferers cannot initiate or maintain directed behavior such as exercise, or are dependent on others to travel. Thus, they cannot attend organized fitness programs. Already carrying heavy burdens, their caregivers may not be inclined to structure and supervise systematic exercise sessions. Regardless, even the oldest, least fit, and cognitively impaired person can accrue benefits from exercise.[38,39] For example, Alzheimer's disease sufferers wander less, are more verbally appropriate, and generally improve with exercise.[40] Assessment by an occupational therapist is one way to identify an appropriate exercise program. Occupational therapists will also teach caregivers how to engage the dementia patient in an exercise program. The following is a list of red flags for exercise:

- Severe heart disease (unstable coronary artery disease or recent myocardial infarction, congestive heart failure with progression to dyspnea, tachyarrhythmias induced by activity, and critical stenosis)
- Immediate hypoxic period following a pulmonary emboli
- Retinal detachment
- Cervical spinal conditions
- Sedentary diabetics who initiate exercise must be monitored carefully, because increased activity will lower glucose levels[2,41] (see Exhibit 4.2.)

EXHIBIT 4.2.
Communication: Pharmacists As Exercise Advocates

Pharmacists should be aware of exercise programs for seniors in their communities. If none exist, pharmacists should actively advocate establishment of such programs. No studies clearly document drug-related savings due to improved health after exercise, but it is reasonable to assume that savings will accrue. This might be an area of study for pharmacists looking for research opportunities. Keep the following key points in mind when communicating with older patients about exercise:

Good: Direct the oldest or frailest individuals to low-resistance programs offered in a safe and secure environment. Successful community programs should ensure that convenient parking is available and facilities are safe and attractive.[a]

Seniors who have been sedentary can start a program by walking for 20 minutes three times weekly at their own pace, regardless of how slow that is.[b]

Minimize the gym lingo. Seniors will be less responsive if you talk about "reps" and "abs" and stick with terms such as "repetitions."

Better: Ask elderly patients who are on multiple medications to tell you or their physician *before* they begin exercise programs so you can monitor medications. Insulin doses, asthma medications, and pain medication may need adjustment, and some conditions are exercise red flags. Discuss how small exercise-related improvements can help reduce doses, possibly eliminating some side effects.

Best: Have handouts available so you can tell seniors what kinds of exercise are best for their unique problems. Include the American Automobile Association's brochure called "A Flexibility Fitness Training Package for Improving Older Driver Performance" for seniors whose driving abilities are slipping. Reinforce and reward seniors. As they improve, remind them that they need less insulin, are sleeping better, or are reporting less pain. Finally, practice what you preach. Get out for a thirty-minute walk at lunch, or engage in some other kind of activity after-hours.

[a]Segal RJ, Reid RD, Courneya KS, et al. Resistance exercise in men receiving androgen deprivation therapy for prostate cancer. *J Clin Oncol.* 2003;21:1653-1659.

[b]Resnick B. A seven-step approach to starting an exercise program for older adults. *Patient Educ Couns.* 2000;39:243-252.

CONCLUSION

The sheer number of studies documenting the benefits of exercise is overwhelming. Meta-analysis is helpful. A review of 1,496 elderly subjects from twenty-nine studies concluded that a senior can realize a 14 percent improvement in endurance from as little as thirty minutes of exercise three times per week.[5] Unfortunately, the level (which would be akin to dose) and duration of exercise needed to accrue specific health benefits are less clear than the frequency. It appears that people who engage in long-term resistance training for at least ten years and then stop, return to baseline within five to six years.[42] Often, control subjects are more likely than exercisers to drop out. Might exercise, once started, be its own incentive to continue? The message is clear: Exercise, even moderate in intensity, must be prescribed for the long term.

NOTES

1. Simkin B. Even frail elderly patients can benefit from exercise. *Geriatric Times* July/August 2002. Available at http://www.geriatrictimes.com. Accessed June 6, 2003.

2. Resnick B. A seven-step approach to starting an exercise program for older adults. *Patient Educ Couns.* 2000;39:243-252.

3. Schechtman KB, Ory MC. The effects of exercise on the quality of life of frail older adults: A preplanned meta-analysis of the FICSIT trials. *Ann Behav Med.* 2001;23:186-197.

4. U.S. Agency for Healthcare Research and Quality, CDC. *Physical activity and older Americans: Benefits and strategies.* June 2000. Available at http://www.ahrq.gov/ppip/activity.htm. Accessed June 6, 2003.

5. Green JS, Crouse SF. The effects of endurance training on functional capacity in the elderly: A meta-analysis. *Med Sci Sports Exerc.* 1995;27:920-926.

6. Paffenbarger RS Jr, Hyde RT, Wing AL, et al. Physical activity, all-cause mortality, and longevity of college alumni. *N Engl J Med.* 1986;314:605-613.

7. Buckwalter JA. Decreased mobility in the elderly: the exercise antidote. *Phys Sport Med.* 1997:25. Available at http://www.physsportsmed.com/issues/1997/09sep/buck.htm. Accessed June 6, 2003.

8. Evans WJ. Effects of exercise on senescent muscle. *Clin Orthop.* 2002; 403S:S211-S220.

9. Fiatarone MA, Marks EA, Ryan ND, et. al. High-intensity strength training in nonagenarians. *JAMA* 1990;263:3029-3034.

10. Fiatarone MA, O'Neill EF, Ryan ND, et al. Exercise training and nutritional supplementation for physical frailty in very elderly people. *N Eng J Med.* 1994; 330:1769-1775.

11. Gill TM, Baker DI, Gottschald M, et al. A program to prevent functional decline in physically frail, elderly persons who live at home. *N Eng J Med.* 2002;247: 1068-1074.

12. Hippocrates. *Exercise for Older Adults.* 1997, 11(3):9-10. Available at www.fhma.com/exercise_in_the_elderly.htm.

13. Geloo ZS, Ershler WB. Treatment and management of cancer in the frail elderly. CMEondemand; 2001. Available at CMEondemand.net/OncSpec/insights_tools/OS701_Geloo.html. Accessed March 2004.

14. Center for Disease Control and Prevention. National Center for Injury Prevention and Control. Falls among older adults: Summary of research findings. Washington, DC: NCIPC; 2001. Available at http://cdc.gov/ncipc/duip/Summary OfFalls.htm. Accessed June 6, 2003.

15. Day L, Fildes B, Gordon I, et. al. Randomised factorial trial of falls prevention among older people living in their own homes. *BJM* 2002;235:128-131.

16. Turner LW, Leaver-Dunn D, DiBrezzo R, et al. Physical activity and osteoporotic fracture among the elderly. *J Athlet Train.* 1998;33:207.

17. Burghardt M. Exercise at menopause: A critical difference. *Medscape Women's Health eJournal* 1999;4. Available at http://www.medscape.com. Accessed June 6, 2003.

18. Ettinger WH, Burns R, Messier SP, et al. A randomized trial comparing aerobic exercise and resistance exercise with a health education program in older adults with knee osteoarthritis. *JAMA* 1997;277:25-31.

19. van Barr ME, Dekker J, Oostendorp RA, et. al. Effectiveness of exercise in patients with osteoarthritis or hip or knee: Nine months' follow up. *Am Rheum Dis.* 2001;60:1123-1130.

20. Penninx BJ, Messier SP, Rejeski J, et al. Physical exercise and the prevention of disability in activities of daily living in older persons with osteoarthritis. *Arch Intern Med.* 2001;161:1309-2316.

21. Brosse AL, Sheets ES, Lett HS, et al. Exercise and the treatment of clinical depression in adults: Recent findings and future directions. *Sports Med.* 2002;32: 741-760.

22. Kasch FW, Boyer JL, Schmidt PK, et al. Ageing of the cardiovascular system during 33 years of aerobic exercise. *Age Ageing* 1999;28:531-536.

23. Blumenthal JA, Emery CF, Madden DJ, Coleman RE, et al. Effects of exercise training on cardiorespiratory function in men and women older than 60 years of age. *Am J Cardiol.* 1991;67:633-639.

24. Park SK, Park JH, Kwon YC, et al. The effect of long-term aerobic exercise on maximal oxygen consumption, left ventricular function and serum lipids in elderly women. *J Physiol Anthropol Appl Human Sci.* 2003;22:11-17.

25. Stratton JR, Levy WC, Cerqueira MD, Schwartz RS, et al. Cardiovascular responses to exercise; Effects of aging and exercise training in healthy men. *Circulation* 1994;89:1648-1655.

26. Yan H, Kuroiwa A, Tanaka H, et al. Effect of moderate exercise on immune senescence in men. *Eur J Appl Physiol.* 2001;86:105-111.

27. Fahlman M, Boardley D, Flynn MG, et al. Effects of endurance training on selected parameters of immune function in elderly women. *Gerontology* 2000;46: 97-104.

28. Woods JA, Lowder TW, Keylock KT. Can exercise training improve immune function in the aged? *Ann N Y Acad Sci.* 2002;959:117-127.

29. Schwartz AL, Mori M, Gao R, et al. Exercise reduces daily fatigue in women with breast cancer receiving chemotherapy. *Med Sci Sports Exerc.* 2001;33:718-723.

30. Fairey AS, Courneya KS, Field CJ, et al. Physical exercise and immune system function in cancer survivors: A comprehensive review and future directions. *Cancer* 2002;94:539-551.

31. Woods JA, Ceddia MA, Wolters BW, et al. Effects of six months of moderate aerobic exercise training on immune function in the elderly. *Mech Ageing Dev.* 1999;109:1-19.

32. Segal RJ, Reid RD, Courneya KS, et al. Resistance exercise in men receiving androgen deprivation therapy for prostate cancer. *J Clin Oncol.* 2003;21:1653-1659.

33. U.S. Department of Health and Human Services, National Institute of Aging. *Exercise: A Guide from the National Institute of Aging.* Washington, DC: NIH, 2001. NIH Publication No. 10-4258.

34. Dunn AL, Trivedi MH, O'Neal HA. Physical activity dose-response effects on outcomes of depression and anxiety. *Med Sci Sports Exerc.* 2001;33(6 Suppl.): S587-597.

35. U.S. Department of Health and Human Services, Center for Disease Control and Prevention. *Physical Activity and Health: A Report of the Surgeon General.* Washington, DC: CDC, 1999. Available at http://www.cdc.gov/nccdphp/sgr/ ataglan.htm. Accessed June 6, 2003.

36. Naylor E, Penev PD, Orbeta L, et al. Daily social and physical activity increases slow-wave sleep and daytime neuropsychological performance in the elderly. *Sleep* 2000;23:87-95.

37. Young-McCaughan S, Mays MZ, Arzola SM, et al. Research and commentary: Change in exercise tolerance, activity and sleep patterns, and quality of life in patients with cancer participating in a structured exercise program. *Oncol Nurs Forum.* 2003;30:441-454.

38. Buchner DM, deLateur BJ. The importance of skeletal muscle strength to physical function in older adults. *Ann Behav Med.* 1992;13:91-98.

39. Fiatarone MA. Physical activity and functional independence in aging. *Res Q Exerc Sport.* 1996;67(3 Suppl.):S70.

40. Arkin SM. Elder rehab: A student-supervised exercise program for Alzheimer's patients. *Gerontologist* 1999;39:729-735.

41. Heath JM, Stuart MR. Prescribing exercise for frail elders. *J Am Board Fam Pract.* 2002;12:218-228.

42. Powell F. Systematic circuit weight training slows physical aging by several years: A 10-year study. *Res Quarter for Exerc Sport.* 2003;74:A8. Available at http://aahperd.confex.com/2003/finalprogram/paper_4099.htm. Accessed June 6, 2003.

Chapter 5

Lifestyle Drugs: Enhancing Life or Eradicating Ugliness?

A woman took her heavily freckled young grandson to the zoo. Soon they joined lots of other children who were waiting in line for face painting.

"You've got so many freckles, there's no place to paint! You need to see a doctor and get rid of those spots!" said the nasty little girl in line in front him. Embarrassed, the grandson started to cry.

His grandmother felt terrible and knelt down to comfort him. "I love your freckles," she said. "When I was a little girl I always wanted freckles. Freckles are beautiful!"

The grandson looked up hopefully. "Really?" he asked.

"Of course!" said the grandmother. "Why, just tell me one thing that's prettier than freckles?"

The grandson thought for a moment, peering intensely into his grandma's face. Softly, he replied, "Wrinkles."

In 2002, the *British Medical Journal* surveyed physicians and asked them to rate a list of . . . well, things . . . as "nondiseases." They concurred with Grandma; freckles appeared as number seven on the list, preceded by work, boredom, bags under the eyes, ignorance, and baldness, and followed by big ears, gray or white hair, and ugliness.[1] Yet, many of these "things" have been treated as medical problems at one time or another. For a brief discussion of this phenomenon, see Exhibit 5.1.

Medical practitioners and payers are in the midst of a similar debate. Traditionally, we have dealt with blatantly medical treatments. Now, new drugs offer unforeseen results[2] and a broader array of out-

EXHIBIT 5.1.
Then and Now: Leopards Changing Their Spots

In the earliest decades of the nineteenth century, people developed dental caries frequently. Dentists used what are now considered rudimentary, even barbaric, tools to fill cavities and pull teeth. The perfect bite was far more the exception than the rule. Over the decades, interventions spurred controversy. Communities resisted fluoridation of water and people grumbled that the investment of thousands of dollars for braces was money wasted for cosmetics. Today, we know that fluoridation has reduced the incidence of cavities significantly, braces improve overall oral health while they eventually improve self-esteem, and dental disease can be correlated to poor nutrition and systemic disease (see Chapter 2).

Conversely, several diseases have succumbed to scientific scrutiny and disappeared from medical texts.[a] Consider chlorosis, first described by Lange in the sixteenth century as an anemia common in adolescent girls and young women. The skin of affected females often took on a greenish hue. Beginning in the seventeenth century, chlorosis was treated with iron supplements. Many physicians believed that it was a result of a nervous disorder affecting various organ systems, including the blood-forming organs. After World War I, the incidence of chlorosis declined, and the disease ceased to be reported in the 1930s. In retrospect, it appears that the "disease" was caused by tightly laced corsets that forced bile into the dermis.[b,c]

[a]Wessely S. What do you think is a non-disease? Pros and cons of medicalisation. *BMJ.* 2002;324:912.

[b]Guggenheim KY. Chlorosis: The rise and disappearance of a nutritional disease. *J Nutr.* 1995;125:1822-1825.

[c]Starobinski J. Chlorosis – the "green sickness." *Psychol Med.* 1981; 11:459-468

comes targeting conditions that seem more cosmetic than medical. Their benefit: by altering a perceived inadequacy, they deliver happiness or improve comfort for the people who use them, but due to some risks, are available only by prescription.

The definition of "normal" is narrowing. Third-party payers, under pressure to create policies attractive to policy holders, must now balance responsible allocation of scarce resources with policies that make policy holders attractive![2] Depending on who is discussing them, this particular set of drugs might be described as cosmetic, life-enhancing, recreational, convenience, quality-of-life, discretionary, or (most commonly) lifestyle drugs.[3,4]

Specific concerns abound and include the perceptions that medical authority is losing ground and abdicating prescribing decisions to patients[5]; that giving natural conditions diagnostic names is an intervention in itself, conferring cost and benefit[2]; and that the word patient—which technically means a person who is ill or under treatment for a disease—does not apply to folks who use drugs to treat nondiseases.[6] Elmer Fudd summed it up: "Disease is a vewy slippery concept." And he added, "So is medicine."

WHAT ARE LIFESTYLE DRUGS?

So, what do you call a group of drugs used to treat nondiseases? Organized medicine is looking for a definition, but without the benefit of a standard word or phrase to start with. The word "medicine" implies a therapeutic remedy. Typically, we call these drugs "lifestyle drugs," but the term elicits reactions ranging from outright objection to misunderstanding.

Some people consider the term inaccurate or misleading because all drugs affect lifestyle or quality of life. Antibiotics and antihistamines/decongestants, agents that are not generally considered lifestyle drugs, relieve discomfort and allow people to resume normal activity. Migraine headaches disrupt lifestyle without threatening lives, yet drugs used to treat migraines are never considered lifestyle drugs when insurers debate coverage. Distinguishing among categories of drugs using terms like symptomatic relief, chronic or acute treatment, or potentially life-threatening intervention is better.

The term *medicalization* has been crafted to describe the propensity for health care professionals to take ownership of a lifestyle problem by defining it as a condition, in the manufacturer's marketing campaign,[3] at the policymaking level, or at the direct care level.[2,7] Critics of these campaigns claim that their authors provide little to no education to patients or prescribers about the difference between treatments that are useful and those that are unnecessary. Medicalization of cosmetic issues creates blurry boundaries; the line between life-enhancing and outright cosmetic is sometimes unclear. Consider an antifungal used to treat a nail fungus. In a teenager its use may primarily be cosmetic. For immunocompromised people, antifungal treatment may save lives. Every drug—and patient complaint—must be evaluated on its own merits. For information on expectations versus reality regarding drugs, see Exhibit 5.2.

Several informal definitions for lifestyle drugs exist. These include

- drugs that are not medically necessary,[3]
- drugs that confer no health benefit, are not indicated for any medical condition, and have no medical indication,[8]
- drugs that if not taken, do not result in additional health risk,[9]
- treatments that increase patient satisfaction, but without which they could live,[10]
- drugs used to treat indications that are personal choice rather than physician-diagnosed illness, or to treat problems that impact health and wellness only marginally,[7] and
- products that improve perceived quality of life without improving medical outcomes or reducing overall health care costs.

So, again, what are these drugs? The answer depends on a number of factors, including indication for the drug, location of the patient or payer, availability of alternative treatments, and cost. The following is a list of a few drugs sometimes considered lifestyle drugs (many more are in the pharmaceutical development pipeline):

- Anabolic steroids
- Antidepressants
- Bed wetting prevention
- Botulism toxin
- Cognition-enhancing drugs
- Erectile dysfunction treatments
- Growth hormone
- Hair growth agents
- Infertility drugs
- Morning-after pills
- Nail fungus treatments
- Nonsedating antihistamines
- Oral contraceptive pills
- Oral influenza-shortening agents
- Smoking cessation products
- Topical antiaging agents
- Weight loss products

EXHIBIT 5.2.
Too Late Now: Expectation versus Reality

Sometimes, patients have unrealistic expectations from drugs. Their hopeful pursuit of youthfulness may cause them to ask fewer questions or abandon their usual cautious approach to medication. Counsel caution when certain drugs are prescribed under the following conditions:

- Anabolic steroids (used to bulk up a frail person's physique or stimulate appetite) in men who have prostatic hypertrophy or prostate cancer;
- Benzodiazepines (used to elevate mood or induce sleep) in people who have a history of falls or disinhibition;
- Buproprion (as a mood elevator or for smoking cessation) in people who have hepatic impairment;
- Finasteride or minoxidil in any patient whose hair is gone completely, and has been for quite some time;
- St. John's wort in any patient who has hepatotoxicity, is taking other drugs that may cause haptotoxicity, or is taking digoxin, warfarin, theophylline, cyclosporine, or protease inhibitors;
- Orlistat or sibutramine (for obesity or weight loss) in any patient who is on multiple medications;
- Sildenafil or tadalafil in men with a history of significant cardiac disease or those who are taking nitrates; and
- Vardenafil in any man who is taking alpha-blockers, nitrates, or nitric oxide donors.

Disagreement about which of these drugs are medically necessary and which are purely cosmetic is to be expected. Some plans do not cover anorectics or cosmetics and may not cover smoking cessation products. However, many private plans do cover these products and more. Profoundly unscientific, arguments include more than medical research; emotion, politics, and finance also fuel decisions.[4]

LIFESTYLE DRUGS: PROFIT OR EXPENSE?

For manufacturers, lifestyle drugs represent untapped pools of potentially giant profit.[11] Lifestyle drug availability is exploding and is often profit driven.[1,11] Critics accuse the pharmaceutical industry of callousness—focusing solely on profitable diseases and conditions—supported by statistics like this: From 1975 to 1997, only 13 of 1,223 new medications listed treatment of deadly tropical diseases common in the Third World.[12] They argue that funds appropriated to lifestyle conditions would be better spent on "real" and life-threatening diseases. So great is the lifestyle drug market, these drugs (especially the erectile dysfunction, anti-obesity, and human growth-hormone agents) dominate the illegal drug trade.[13]

When drugs are medically unnecessary, drug development's companion is marketing. Industry campaigns may try to redefine consumers' understanding of illness[7] or use direct-to-consumer (DTC) marketing to stimulate demand.[9,10,14] DTC advertising may discourage consumers from stoically enduring their freckles (or whatever) and encourage them to resolve mundane issues aggressively with drugs; it may also underplay risks.[15] Branding and marketing generate the perception of quality and brand loyalty,[14] generate positive perceptions about safety,[10] and remind patients to refill prescriptions.[10] Patients' demands, driven by longer life spans, new technology, and greater expectations, often appear insatiable.[4]

MANAGING LIFESTYLE DRUGS

What can we do when seniors want a lifestyle drug? The pharmacist's role is to ensure that patients are well-informed and risks are minimized. True informed consent has six parts; using the template in Exhibit 5.3 can ensure that patients have all the information they need (this template actually serves for any counseling, not just lifestyle drug counseling). And, as always, keep your personal opinion to yourself.

More often than ever, elders use Internet sources to purchase drugs at a savings. Unfortunately, lifestyle drugs are among those most likely to be counterfeited and sold via the Internet. That said, watch pharmacy journals and newspapers for articles on counterfeiting trends and warn elders. Tell them that if a drug looks different from what they expect, fails to work, or causes side effects different from what they experienced before or not listed in the prescribing information, they should bring the drug to you or the physician. And, when manufactur-

EXHIBIT 5.3.
Communication: Appropriately Informing Seniors About Lifestyle Drugs

1. Describe the drug and how to use it. For the erectile dysfunction drugs, you might say, "This drug may help men get and keep an erection only when they are sexually excited. Once the sexual activity ends, blood flow to the penis decreases and the erection goes away. This drug will not cure erectile dysfunction. This medicine usually begins to work within X minutes after taking it. It continues to work for up to Y hours."
2. Explain possible risks or discomforts in layman's terms. For example, you might say, "While using tretinoin creams and lotions, keep exposure to sunlight, including sunlamps, to a minimum. If you have a sunburn, discontinue the tretinoin until you have fully recovered. Use sunscreen products (at least SPF 15) and protective clothing over treated areas when you cannot avoid exposure to the sun. Avoid wind and cold extremes of weather, too, because they may be irritating."
3. Describe the potential benefits and when to expect results. For topical minoxidil, say (pausing between bits of information), "Minoxidil works differently in every person. For some people, it doesn't work at all, and no one can expect 100 percent regrowth. (pause) Chances of success are best if you have been losing your hair for a short time or have little initial hair loss. (pause) It usually takes about four months for regular-strength minoxidil to begin producing regrowth. Minoxidil Extra Strength may begin working in as little as two months. (pause) Women see best results in approximately eight months; for men, up to a year is required. (pause) To keep the new hair, you must continue using the product. If you stop, you will probably lose the regrown hair within three to four months."
4. List alternatives, if any exist. For smoking cessation products, you might talk about the gum (which is not the best choice for denture wearers), the spray, the patch, and buproprion (see Chapter 6, "Addiction").
5. Talk about when a call to the prescriber or pharmacy is prudent. For orlistat, point out that patients should call their physician if they experience bloody or cloudy urine; change in hearing; unusual or contagious diarrhea; difficult, frequent, or painful urination; or earache.
6. Discuss how to discontinue the treatment. For drugs like benzodiazepines, abrupt cessation can cause withdrawal. Tell patients to talk to their physicians before stopping benzodiazepines abruptly.

ers provide patient information leaflets, be sure to pass them along to the patient and ascertain that they can read and understand them. If seniors bring drugs to you that appear to be counterfeit, contact the Food and Drug Administration (FDA) MedWatch Program at 1-800-FDA-1088.

LOCATION, LOCATION, LOCATION

Use of lifestyle drugs is an issue of philosophy and culture.[2,11,16] Depending on the area of the country and the predominant culture, certain drugs may or may not be considered lifestyle drugs. Consider that in Japan, fluoxetine (Prozac) is considered a lifestyle drug.[16] How will society regard drugs for shyness[8] or new substance P-inhibitors that do not necessarily relieve depression but do offer a pick-me-up?[11]

Generally, younger generations are the heaviest users of lifestyle drugs, but as the youth-cherishing baby boomers become eligible for AARP membership, we can expect to see more seniors using lifestyle drugs. B. G. Charlton, in his article "The Potential for Pharmacological Treatment of Unpleasant Psychological Symptoms to Increase Personal Fulfillment in Old Age,"[17] indicates that with aging, people experience a decline in personal fulfillment and emotional blunting. He suggests that moderate and occasional use of alcohol or benzodiazepines would let elders respond better. (He also acknowledges that these drugs are not without contraindications in elderly populations, and it is these effects that contribute to their popularity and abuse.[17]) Others have suggested that medicine is now moving into the realm of palliating low-grade misery.[15]

In elderly patients in particular, a concern about intensifying the already prevalent polypharmacy problem is most important. Polypharmacy often follows incremental prescribing to treat symptoms and adverse events caused by other drugs. If the patient, using only a mirror as a diagnostic tool, pressures precribers to add lifestyle drugs to a heavy drug regimen, the potential for misadventure is compounded.[6,15]

COST, SAFETY, AND CONFIDENTIALITY

Safety and cost are certainly driving forces, leading most insurers to ration lifestyle drugs. Most insurance plans do not provide unlimited coverage of "expensive blue pills" or similar high-cost medications,[2] and others use screening devices to ensure that safety issues are addressed from the start. Specific concerns about the use of some lifestyle drugs are described in Table 5.1. Note that a few unregulated dietary supplements are included. These drugs, if or when considered as lifestyle enhancers, complicate the picture even further.

Confidentiality expectations are often greater when lifestyle drugs are used than with other drugs. Plan members may be less willing to reveal that they are using a drug to grow hair, cure impotence, or remove wrinkles than to treat hypertension or diabetes. With confidentiality in general becoming an increasingly important issue, this is a major consideration for health care providers.

CONCLUSION

When conditions are not life-threatening or treatments offer only neutral or tentative benefit, discussion, debate, and rationing are reasonable. Drugs and treatments that seem to be lifestyle agents on one level, such as smoking cessation and obesity drugs, may in the long run offer hidden and important improvements, as did the dental interventions cited in Exhibit 5.1.

Richard Russo wrote *Empire Falls,* a work of fiction based in the Maine town of the same name. He described the people of Empire Falls as normal people with all the usual blemishes and warts, unlike people in certain parts of California, who had "eradicated ugliness." It remains to be seen whether drugs and technology will indeed eradicate ugliness, or whether improvements that now seem cosmetic will lead to better overall wellness.

NOTES

1. Smith R. In search of non-disease. *BMJ* 2002;324:883-885.
2. Greene J. Al wants more hair, less fat and a better life . . . and he wants his health plan to pay for it. *Hospital and Health Networks* 1999;73:36-40.

TABLE 5.1. Lifestyle Drug Considerations in Elderly Patients

Medication	Approved Use	Potential Lifestyle Use	Concern in Elderly Patients
Anabolic steroids	Anemia, hereditary angioedema, metastatic breast cancer	Poor appetite, failure to thrive	Geriatric patients treated with anabolic steroids may be at increased risk for developing prostatic hypertrophy and prostatic carcinoma.
Ascorbic acid	Scurvy, urinary acidification	Cold prevention, aging retardation, other indications	Diabetic patients, patients prone to recurrent renal calculi, those undergoing fecal occult blood tests, and those on sodium-restricted diets or anticoagulant therapy should not take excessive doses of vitamin C over an extended period of time.
Benzodiazepines	Anxiety, seizure disorders, muscle relaxation	Personal fulfillment, alleviation of emotional blunting, low-grade misery	Ataxia, excessive sedation, dizziness, confusion, and hypotension can occur, increasing fall risk. Significant addiction potential. Initiate doses at the lowest possible level and titrate slowly.
Bupropion	Depression, smoking cessation	Smoking cessation	The risk of toxic reaction to this drug may be greater in patients with impaired renal function.
Erythropoietin	Anemia	Performance enhancement, fatigue	An increased incidence of mortality in patients with cardiac disease and increased incidence of thrombotic events have been reported. Resumption of menses may occur in some female patients.

Finasteride	Regrowth of hair	Regrowth of hair	Generally ineffective if hair loss is not recent.
Fish oil			Malabsorption syndromes
Human growth hormone	Growth failure in children, cathexia	Aging retardation, weight loss, fatigue and asthenia, wrinkle removal, sexual performance enhancement, memory aid	May enhance the proliferation of diabetic retinopathy (based on in vitro studies). Because of the diabetogenic effect of growth hormone, it should be given with care to patients with diabetes mellitus; adjustment of antidiabetic therapy may be necessary. Hypothyroidism may develop during treatment.
Minoxidil	Hypertension	Regrowth of hair	Topical minoxidil works best before substantial hair loss occurs.
Orlistat	Obesity	Weight loss	Magnitude of weight loss was modest, and the long-term health benefits and safety remain unclear. Vitamin deficiencies are possible.
St. John's wort		Depression, malaise	Potential for multiple drug interactions
Sibutramine	Obesity	Weight loss	Substantially increases blood pressure in some patients. Dose selection for an elderly patient should be cautious, reflecting the greater frequency of decreased hepatic, renal, or cardiac function; concomitant disease; or other drug therapy.

TABLE 5.1 (continued)

Medication	Approved Use	Potential Lifestyle Use	Concern in Elderly Patients
Sildenafil	Erectile dysfunction	Enhancement of the normal sexual response	Administration with nitrates (either regularly and/or intermittently) and nitric oxide donors increases risk of hypotension. Geriatrics (65 years and older), men with CrCl less than 30 mL/min, and men with hepatic failure use an initial dose of 25 mg. Dose adjustments are needed if the patient is taking concomitant CYP3A4 inhibitors.
Selective serotonin reuptake inhibitors	Depression, anxiety, muscle relaxation	Compulsive shopping, social anxiety	Lower initial doses or longer dosing intervals are recommended in people older than 65.
Tadalafil	Erectile dysfunction	Enhancement of the normal sexual response	Potentiates the hypotensive effect of nitrates. Coadministration with alpha-blockers other than 0.4 mg/day tamsulosin is contraindicated. Dose adjustments are needed if the patient has renal or hepatic impairment or is taking concomitant CYP3A4 inhibitors.
Testosterone replacement therapy	Congenital or acquired hypogonadism	Fatigue, malaise, impotence	Increases prostate cancer risk.
Vardenafil	Erectile dysfunction	Enhancement of the normal sexual response	Coadministration with alpha-blockers, nitrates, or nitric oxide donor drugs is not advised. Geriatrics (65 years and older) and patients with hepatic failure use an initial dose of 5 mg once daily. Dose adjustments are needed if the patient is taking concomitant CYP3A4 inhibitors.

3. Sevon M, Mitrany D. Quality of life drugs: Framing the issue. Available at www.amcp.org/public/pubs/journal/vol5/num3/spotlight.html. Accessed June 1, 2001.

4. Frankel S, Ebrahim S, Davey Smith G. The limits to demand for health care. *BMJ* 2000;321(7252):40-45.

5. Wessely S. What do you think is a non-disease? Pros and cons of medicalisation. *BMJ* 2002;324:912.

6. Flower R. Lifestyle drugs: Pharmacology and the social agenda. *Trends in Pharmacological Sciences* 2004;25:182-185.

7. Gilbert D, Walley T, New B. Lifestyle medicines. *BMJ* 2000; 321:1341-1344.

8. Laurance J. Health: Should self-esteem be available at NHS? *Independent* 2001;9.

9. Overman S. Warning: Viagra may cause headaches for health insurers. *HR Magazine* January 9, 1998.

10. Go on, it's good for you. *The Economist* August 8, 1998:348.

11. Gunsauley C. Golden age of rx development involves plenty of green. *Employee Benefit News* 1998.

12. Silverstein K. Millions for Viagra, pennies for diseases of the poor: Research money goes to profitable lifestyle drugs. *The Nation* 1999; 269:13-18.

13. On the trail of the World-Wide Web of fake lifestyle drugs. *Sofia Morning News* January 18, 2004. Available at http://novinite.com/newsleter/print.php?id=30027. Accessed November 9, 2004.

14. Hallahan M, Madell R. Media mix: Your monthly window on pharmaceutical marketing; Rx branding: A brand new culture. *Pharmaceutical Executive* 1999;19:98-100.

15. Walley T. Lifestyle medicines and the elderly. *Drugs Aging* 2002;19:163-168.

16. Japanese consumers: Feeling sorry for themselves. *The Economist* April 10, 1999:351.

17. Charlton BG. The potential for pharmacological treatment of unpleasant psychological symptoms to increase personal fulfillment in old age. *QJM* 2001;94:333-336.

Chapter 6

Addiction

A recently widowed woman went to see a spiritualist. The spiritualist asked how the husband had died, and the wife reported chronic obstructive pulmonary disease. His continued smoking had sapped his last breath. "Well, that explains the message he's sending—please send him a pack of cigarettes."

"I don't know where to send them," the wife said.

"Why not?" asked the spiritualisst.

"Well, he didn't say he's in heaven, but I can't imagine he'd be in hell."

The spiritualist paused, then said: "Well, he didn't mention anything about including matches in the package."

Difficult to break, patterns of addiction follow many seniors into senescence and often lead to an early demise. Currently, around 1 percent of elders use illicit drugs. Alcohol is the most serious abuse issue among them,[1] with approximately 5 million seniors (10 percent) having problems.[2-5] Addiction in seniors is often hard to spot, because they live alone, are retired (and thus have no work-related problems), and receive fewer driving citations.[4] Almost one-third of older alcoholics develop their problem late in life.[6]

Unlike younger people, elders who seek addiction treatment are usually self-referred.[1] Often, however, mental health services and addiction issues in general are stigmatizing for older adults, which serves to discourage them from seeking treatment.[7]

Drug and substance abuse are often associated with youth, but the generation most closely identified with a youthful image—the baby boomers—will all turn 60 by 2020. Thus, experts expect rates of abuse of and addiction to illicit drugs to double by 2020.[8] Some ex-

Pharmacy Practice in an Aging Society
© 2006 by The Haworth Press, Inc. All rights reserved.
doi:10.1300/5404_06

perts, however, believe that, even at the present, substance abuse among seniors is an invisible epidemic, because if prescription and over-the-counter drug abuse is considered, nearly 20 percent of elders have addiction or abuse problems.[3,4] Families may miss the signs of addiction, which are listed here.

Cognitive	Behavioral
Memory loss	Social withdrawal
Depression	Slurred or pressured speech
Mood swings	Evasiveness
Irritability	Unexplained motor vehicle accidents
Decreased concentration	Falls[4]
Suicidal ideation	

They may also attribute them to normal aging.[4] Often, the problem remains unidentified until a fall or an automobile accident sends the senior to the emergency department.[6] (Of elders seen in emergency departments, 12 to 14 percent are problem drinkers.[9-11])

RIGHT UNDER YOUR NOSE: LEGAL DRUG ABUSE

For our purposes, "legal drug abuse" (LDA) will be defined as the "use of a prescription or OTC drug by a person other than for whom it was prescribed, or for nonmedical purposes."[12] This definition is used commonly by the law enforcement community. LDA often starts because seniors consider prescription drugs, OTC medications, and herbals safe, and compared with illicit drugs, they are.[13] Abuse frequently begins after analgesics are prescribed; and, although pain is the most common symptom associated with LDA,[4,14] laxatives and caffeine are also abused frequently.[4]

Rather than visit a physician, elders use OTC products to self-treat minor illnesses up to 85 percent of the time and use twice as much OTC medication as other age groups.[14] Legal drug abusers may self-diagnose incorrectly, overdose, or overuse medication and develop rebound syndrome.[15] Risk factors for LDA include increasing age, female gender, poor to fair health status, and daily drinking.[15]

LDA may be recreational or therapeutic. Recreational abusers tend to start by using illicit drugs socially in their youth. Over the years, however, they tend to hide their abuse and addiction and turn to legal and more readily available drugs to self-medicate. Therapeutic abusers, on the other hand, begin quietly, with legally obtained prescriptions, and become more secretive as they develop a habit. Often, they invent ailments as an excuse for using more medication.[16] Tips on how to communicate with senior abusers or addicts can be found in Exhibit 6.1.

Opioids, central nervous system (CNS) stimulants, and CNS depressants are the most commonly abused prescription drugs, in general and by seniors.[12] The Drug Abuse Warning Network indicates

---

EXHIBIT 6.1.
Communication: Communicating with Senior Abusers or Addicts

Be direct about your concerns. Do not sugarcoat or dance around the facts, and support your facts with good records. Simply say, "You have had your prescription refilled early three times, and I cannot refill it early again," or support your statements similarly with statistics or your observation of behaviors.

Never try to reason with a person who is under the influence. Instead, indicate that you need to reschedule the discussion to a later time.

Avoid using the words "drug addict"; these have a strong stigma for seniors.

Avoid emotional confrontation; understand that seniors are often angry about their problem and consider it a moral failure. If an addict becomes abusive, establish boundaries. Say, "I will not allow you to call me names," or, "I will call the police if you continue to cause a disturbance." And do it.

Do not counsel family members or concerned others to throw away the substance of abuse. This rarely works.

Offer a "brown bag day" when seniors can bring all of their medications to the pharmacy and chat in an informal setting.

Review the labels of prescription and OTC medications and ask elders whether they are able to read the small print (see Chapter 3 for tips on dealing with the visually impaired).

Identify addiction support groups in your area, such as Pills Anonymous (http://pillsanonymous.com), and make patients aware of them.

Sources: Colvin R. *Prescription Drug Addiction: The Hidden Epidemic.* Omaha, NE: Addicus Books; 2002; Sitzman K. Over-the-counter medications – use caution! *AAOHN J.* 2003;51(12):544.

that emergency department visits related to prescription narcotic analgesics doubled between 1994 and 2001.[17] Among OTC products, laxatives, decongestants, and antihistamines are most frequently abused.

Patients have many supply routes for their drug of choice. Often, they badger prescribers into writing legitimate prescriptions. Other sources are theft, employee diversion, ordering via the Internet, veterinary pharmacies, and prescription fraud.[17] And, interestingly enough, the National Drug Information Center now lists "pill ladies" as street slang for older women who sell their prescription drugs to augment their income. Watch for them.

NICOTINE

Many seniors smoke heavily, justifying their habit with emotionally compelling arguments like, "It's the only pleasure I have left," or, "After forty years, it's too late to stop." But at any age, smoking cessation benefits smokers and the people around them (see Exhibit 2.1 Cutting Edge: Secondhand Smoke—An End to the Controversy?).

Most elders began smoking as adolescents, long before smoking's hazards were clear.[18] Up to the middle of the twentieth century, it was not unusual for children of twelve or fourteen to become addicted to cigarettes. National campaigns with a special emphasis on children (but inclusive of others) have reduced the rate of smoking from 37.4 percent in 1970 to 24.7 percent in 2000.[19]

Regardless, approximately 4.5 million adults older than sixty-five, primarily men, still smoke.[20] Almost three-quarters of the 419,000 deaths attributed to smoking in 1990 occurred in people older than sixty-five.[21] Older smokers think differently than younger smokers do. More likely to be heavy smokers with serious addiction,[22] they confuse smoking-related health problems with aging,[23,24] consider smoking's effects reversible,[24] and link the habit with weight control and coping benefits.[25]

Unit-dose nicotine (cigarettes) causes considerable damage. Toxin-laded cigarette smoke stimulates respiratory polymorphonuclear leukocytes to create free radicals and oxidants, causing lipid peroxidation and inflammation.[20,26] Smokeless chewing tobacco, once more a growing problem, delivers nicotine equivalent to three to four cigarettes over thirty minutes[20] directly to the sensitive oral muscosa.

Without intoxication or impairment, nicotine calms smokers by increasing norepinephrine levels.[20] Nicotine addicts report decreased aggression, improved focus on cognitive tasks, better vigilance, improved weight control, and elevated mood.[27]

Prevention and cessation efforts have tended to ignore older smokers.[28] Even after age sixty-five, however, smoking cessation can decrease risk of myocardial infarction, death from congestive heart failure, and lung cancer. Smoking-induced illnesses abate or heal more quickly, and cerebral circulation improves.[29] Smoking cessation also slows ventilatory decline. The Fletcher-Peto model of lung function decline with smoking, the gold standard for evaluating cessation, shows that until age eighty, smoking cessation leads to a return to normal (and more gradual) rate of decline. This improvement is more pronounced in women.[26,30]

Many of the 44 percent of older smokers who would like to quit[22] think it is too late or too difficult at their age. When engaging older smokers, pharmacists can use these guidelines:

- Never suggest smoking cessation to seriously ill or recently bereaved elders.[24]
- Acknowledge that people with histories of mental illness or addictions have unique (and difficult) issues and may have greater difficulty quitting.[20]
- Tailor older smokers' efforts to their individual concerns.

Helping Seniors Quit Smoking

A physician's suggestion increases cessation rates, but physicians are less likely to advise geriatric smokers to quit.[31] Short (ten-minute) counseling sessions from any health care professional also significantly increase cessation,[20,26] and clinical teamwork seems to work best.[28] Most older smokers are receptive to intervention.[21]

Certain approaches have been proven to work well and can be adapted for the older smoker.[20,32] Consider the "five As" of smoking cessation intervention:

1. *Ask* about tobacco use at each contact.
2. *Advise* seniors to quit.
3. *Assess* willingness to quit.

4. Assist using counseling and pharmacotherapy.
5. Arrange follow-up contact, preferably within one week of the quit date.[29,33,34]

For elders, the asking step is crucial. They are probably experiencing health consequences of smoking and see health care providers more often than do younger adults.[21] Simple steps can heighten your awareness of who among your clientele or patient population smokes or chews, and lay a foundation for subsequent action. Adding smoking status to an inpatient facility's vital sign list increases the occurrence of the ask step of intervention by 32 percent.[32] Applying a bright chart sticker identifying residents as smokers also increases intervention.[35]

Ready . . .

Compared with younger smokers, smokers older than fifty are less likely to want to quit.[23] Asking patients at each contact whether they smoke lets them know that this issue remains crucial. Clinicians can use the following "five R's" to reinforce information with smokers who hesitate to quit:

1. *R*elevance: Encourage elders to describe why quitting would be personally relevant.
2. *R*isks: Help them identify the most visible or immediate negative effects of tobacco use: bad breath, stained teeth, dirty ashtrays, emphysema, or a recent stroke.
3. *R*ewards: Ask elders to envision how life would improve without tobacco.
4. *R*oadblocks: Help them realistically identify barriers to smoking cessation, such as withdrawal and anxiety.
5. *R*epetition: Repeat the message, even after the cessation process has begun.[29,33,34]

Relevance. Social pressure, inconvenience, and smoking-related symptoms often motivate young smokers to quit. After years of smoking, however, elders may ignore social pressure, fabricate positive benefits, or identify symptoms (fatigue, congestion, lack of energy, weakness, and coughing) as signs of normal aging. To improve their readiness to quit, help elders see health benefits, identify three or more smoking-related symptoms or problems they have had within the past week, and comprehend their loved ones' desire for them to quit.[23] Discussing tobacco's outrageous cost may also motivate them to make an attempt at quitting.

Risks. Remind older smokers that their pack-year history puts them at greatest risk for smoking-related catastrophe.[27] Carefully explain smoking's effects on all bodily systems, especially its relationship to cancer and upper respiratory health. Stress smoking's role in six of the fourteen leading causes of death.[28] And, if the smoker complains about the cost of multiple medications, bluntly describe smoking's effect on drug metabolism. Dosages of anticonvulsants, betablockers, caffeine, clozapine, fluvoxamine, insulin, olanzapine, and theophylline can often be reduced after smoking cessation.

Rewards. When counseling older smokers, present rewards in a balanced way. Acknowledge that this pleasurable habit perpetuates more smoking (twenty or more cigarettes a day is about average) because nicotine changes neurotransmitter levels reliably, accessibly, and positively in less than ten seconds.[27]

Powerfully emphasize that the rewards of cessation exceed that pleasure. For example, at age seventy, smokers have a 10 percent chance of lung cancer. Quitting at sixty reduces the risk to 6 percent; quitting at fifty reduces it to 4 percent; at forty to 2 percent; and at thirty to 1 percent.[36] In addition, blood pressure and heart rate fall within twenty minutes of the last cigarette. Oxygen and carbon monoxide levels return to normal eight hours later. Risk of heart attack falls within a day and lung function improves 30 percent within three months.[37]

Roadblocks. Withdrawal and the costs of adjunctive treatment can be barriers to smoking cessation. Withdrawal severity will vary depending on pack-years of smoking. Most smokers are familiar with withdrawal's discomfort, since it usually takes six or seven attempts to quit. Withdrawal symptoms can persist for weeks, and elders must brace themselves for this possibility.[26,29]

Adjunctive treatment can be costly in an underhanded way. Consider that nicotine replacement therapy (NRT) costs less than the average pack-a-day habit. But smokers generally buy one or two packs of cigarettes at a time; some smokers have trouble paying for a week's supply of NRT at once.[23] Pharmacists who agree to sell smaller, more affordable quantities help elders quit and also increase their contact with these patients.

Repetition. Repeat the smoking cessation message at every opportunity, always emphasizing that success often takes six or seven attempts.

Set . . .

Once they signal they are ready, help smokers choose an impending quit date and talk about different approaches. Quitting "cold turkey" usually works best, but some elders may prefer tapering.[26] In general, use of NRT doubles the chance an individual will quit smoking;[24] the subsequent success rate in the elderly can approach 20 percent.[38] Discuss coping mechanisms such as chewing gum, sucking sugarless candy, eating low-calorie snacks, or increasing physical activity.[23] Pharmacists should discourage smokers from switching to a low nicotine cigarette. These smokers will increase the numbers of cigarettes smoked or inhale more deeply, creating the same risk as smoking "high test" cigarettes.[23,32]

Go!

Whether adjunctive medications are used or not, telephone counseling can be particularly helpful for older patients, whose mobility is usually limited.[29] Initially, daily calls might be helpful, but as the weeks of abstinence accrue, less frequent contact is needed. The type, intensity, and duration of withdrawal varies from person to person, and among each person's successive cessation attempts. A three-month period of withdrawal or continuing craving is not unusual.

Offer encouragement that is tailored to the smoker, reinforcing reasons for quitting, suggesting ways to deal with slip-ups, or suggesting ways to cope with symptoms. Say, "Every time you have a *insert the specific withdrawal symptom,* its intensity will be less than the last time. Focus on that, not on how awful the symptom is. People who have used nicotine for a long time often find that their minds look for any excuse to relapse."

Choosing between the OTC gum or patch versus the prescription nasal spray or inhaler as an NRT approach raises certain issues in the elderly. Many smokers prefer the gum, as they can control the rate of nicotine release.[26] Denture wearers, of course, may find gum chewing uncomfortable.[20] Nicotine spray and inhalers are useful in that they ease the discomfort of withdrawal and can be used as a supplement to gum or patches for acute symptoms.[26]

Persons with psychiatric illnesses are about twice as likely as the general population to smoke tobacco,[39] and those with schizophrenia are three or four times as likely.[40,41] Researchers think that neurobiological and psychosocial factors reinforce the nicotine use in psychiatric populations.[42,43] Bupropion may be the best alternative for elders with mental health issues to address the neurobiological component.[24] In any elder with renal or hepatic failure or seizure disorders, it should be used extremely cautiously. Start bupropion a week before the quit date; it may be needed for six to twelve weeks. If after seven weeks cessation eludes the smoker, success is unlikely.[26]

Oral or transdermal clonidine in doses ranging from 0.1 to 0.75 mg/day promotes abstinence rates of around 25 percent. Start the drug a few days before the quit date.[38]

As elders progress into "cigarette sobriety," adjust medication doses and celebrate each accomplishment—improved exercise tolerance, the vanished cough, a decreased dose.

ALCOHOL: DRUG OR SOCIAL AMENITY?

Understanding alcohol and alcoholism is like reading a Russian classic—the machinations are staggering: conflicting methodologies, unreliable self-reports, inconsistent definitions of alcohol intake, misdiagnosis of alcohol-related conditions, no linear relationship between health risks and alcohol consumption. Yikes! Then consider that moderate alcohol consumption reduces the risk of several conditions. Should we encourage abstinence or promote moderation? And does abstinence help after years of heavy drinking?

Dependent? Abuser?

The Diagnostic and Statistical Manual of Mental Disorders, Fourth Edition (DSM IV-TR), indicates that alcohol-dependent people meet three of seven criteria. Abusers are people who are not dependent, but who continue drinking despite physical, psychological, social, emotional, or occupational problems.[44] The DSM criteria are listed here:

1. Persistent desire to drink, or unsuccessful attempts at moderation
2. Inability to exercise control over drinking once begun
3. Withdrawal symptoms or avoidance of withdrawal
4. Tolerance—the need to increase intake to experience a high
5. Spending too much time drinking or recovering from drinking
6. Giving up or reducing normal activities in favor of drinking
7. Continuing to drink in the presence of a physical or psychological problem exacerbated by drinking

Men drink more than women. Men born before World War II are 2.4 times more likely to drink than their female peers, and 4.7 times more likely to be alcohol dependent. Men born around the Vietnam era are 1.2 times more likely to drink and 1.4 times more likely to be alcohol dependent than their female peers.[45]

Low versus Moderate?

One drink is 0.5 ounce or 15 grams of alcohol, the equivalent of a 12-ounce beer, 5 ounces of wine, or 1.5 ounces of 80-proof distilled spirits.[9] The U.S. Department of Health and Human Services (DHHS) defines moderate drinking as two drinks daily for men and one drink daily for women. Low and heavy intake is simply consumption below or above moderate levels.[9] Drink for drink, males' blood alcohol levels are lower than females', as they absorb and metabolize alcohol faster and have a larger volume of distribution (Vd). For most men, daily al-

---

cohol intake of 72 ounces of beer, 1 liter of wine, or 8 ounces of distilled spirits daily over twenty years will lead to scarring, fibrosis, and portal vein hypertension. In women, the risk threshold is 50 to 75 percent lower, and elevated risk persists even after abstinence.[46]

The DHHS's National Institute on Alcohol Abuse and Alcoholism recommends no more than one drink daily for people aged sixty-five and older.[9] Seniors' leaner body mass increases sensitivity to alcohol, and even modest consumption can exacerbate existing illnesses and create potential drug interactions. See Exhibit 6.2 for a discussion of alcohol use in nursing homes.

EXHIBIT 6.2.
Ethics on the Spot: Alcohol Use in Nursing Homes

Your customer is worried because her heavy-drinking father has been admitted to a nursing home. She wants to know whether she should bring him a beer or two.

Reliable information about rates of alcohol use disorders and alcohol consumption in nursing homes is scarce. Direct care staff will relate anecdotally that, despite their best efforts, residents, especially those with long-standing alcohol problems, manage to acquire alcoholic beverages and drink actively.

Nursing homes have a range of policies. Some allow residents to keep alcohol in their rooms or will secure a personal supply. Others sponsor cocktail (or nonalcoholic "mocktail") hours to promote social interaction. Still others require a physician-order. And some facilities include permission to imbibe in standing admission orders, requiring a physician's order if alcohol is forbidden. Very few require total abstinence. Frequently, nursing homes have alcohol policies but do not enforce them.

When the nursing home does not provide alcohol, sympathetic family members or friends frequently bring gifts of liquor or agree to fetch it for the resident. Sometimes, residents who have day privileges stock up when they are away from the nursing home or a staff member may act as a supplier.

Advise your customer to talk with her father's attending physician and the nursing home staff to make an informed decision.

Source: Adapted from Klein WC, Jess C. One last pleasure? Alcohol use among elderly people in nursing homes. *Health & Social Work.* 2002;27:193-203.

Begin with the Benefits

Traditionally, researchers associated alcohol with *increased* risk for many conditions. Recent studies, however, have associated low-to-moderate alcohol intake with *lowering* risk for some conditions. The J-shaped alcohol-risk relationship shown in Figure 6.1 demonstrates that starting with the risk for abstainers, risk for some conditions decreases with low-to-moderate alcohol intake and then dramatically increases with heavy intake. So, moderate drinking may be beneficial. Abstainers have higher coronary artery disease and thrombotic disease mortality rates, and moderate drinking potentially improves ulcerative colitis, macular degeneration, and upper respiratory infection.[47-54] However, since moderate drinkers have other, unidentified risk-lowering habits, no one recommends nondrinkers start drinking. See Exhibit 6.3 for a discussion of abstinence versus moderation.

Alcohol abuse and its associated problems decrease with age. Spontaneous remission, treatment interventions, and earlier alcohol-related mortality partially explain the trend. The elderly drink less than their younger counterparts, but the potential problems are significant. See Exhibit 6.4 to compare present-day alcohol consumption with historical data.

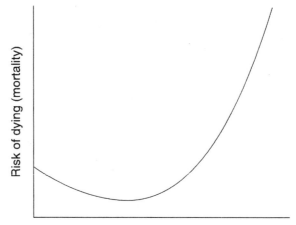

FIGURE 6.1. The J-shaped alcohol-risk relationship

EXHIBIT 6.3.
Total Abstinence versus Controlled Drinking

Most Americans consider alcoholism a progressive, irreversible disease marked by loss of control. Current alcoholism and alcohol abuse treatment models used by U.S. physicians favor harm reduction strategies and total abstinence. Abstinence advocates insist that controlled drinking merely excuses or ignores alcoholism and, eventually, individuals will again drink heavily. They also assert that the damage alcohol use can inflict makes abstinence the only responsible goal.

Many European models allow controlled drinking, citing research findings that up to 75 percent of heavy drinkers do not become chemically dependent. Rather, their problem is abuse. Drinkers indifferent to abstinence often consider controlled drinking an acceptable outcome. Proponents of moderation also suggest that the American medical superstructure has been so focused on abstinence that little funding has been allocated to study moderation.

Many experts now believe that severely dependent drinkers do better with abstinence approaches, but moderation is appropriate for those with moderate problems. Further, many people dislike the twelve-step programs that have been abstinence's cornerstone for decades. For this group, interventions such as contracts, reduction of consumption, and development of coping skills work better.

Often, people reduce alcohol consumption without formal interventions or programs. While studies are scarce, evidence suggests women may control drinking more successfully than do men and that moderate drinking might be an achievable goal for those whose drinking is stress triggered. Until treatment outcomes are better understood, these controversies will continue.

Sources: U.S. Department of Health and Human Services. 10th Report to the U.S. Congress on Alcohol and Health. Washington, DC: NIH; June 2000. Publication No. 00-1583. Shute N, Tangley L. The drinking dilemma. *U.S. News & World Report* September 8, 1997: 123; 9: 54-64. Hersey B. *The controlled drinking dilemma: A review of four decades of acrimony.* New York: Alexander Belucai MD, 1998. Available at: http://www.doctordeluca.com/library/abstinence HR/FourDecadesAcrimony-print.htm. Accessed February 17, 2003.

EXHIBIT 6.4.
***Then and Now:* Prevalence of Drinking**

In general, people today drink less than they did in the past. Per capita consumption of alcohol in the 1780s was triple what it is today. Alcohol sales have declined since the 1980s, and national surveys also reflect decreased consumption. In 1984, for example, 70 percent of the population consumed alcohol, compared with 65 percent in 1990. More recent estimates suggest a further reduction to 54 percent.

Source: Fernandez-Sola J, Garcia G, Elena M, et al. Muscle antioxidant status in chronic alcoholism. *Alcohol Clin Exp Res.* 2002; 26: 1858-1862.

Risks

Alcohol's effects are circular and progressive. Once alcohol assaults the gastrointestinal system and harms the mucosa, vitamin absorption is impaired. Avitaminosis causes neurological damage. Inefficient, ineffective blood synthesis causes anemias that challenge the heart, lungs, and liver. Liver malfunction raises lipids, which causes multiple cardiovascular problems. Escalating and entwining, these problems destroy baseline health and invite infection and a downward spiral of increasingly poor health.

Alcohol is particularly toxic to elders. It has multiple drug interactions and will potentiate sedation caused by prescription drugs, increasing the risk of cogitive impairment and falls. Elders are more likely to be disabled if they have a persistent history of problem drinking. Older alcoholics appear to be at greater risk for suicide (see Chapter 9) than young alcoholic adults.

And what is a drink without a smoke? Concurrent smoking and daily drinking triples the risk of cirrhosis and increases the risk of head and neck cancer.[9]

The Pharmacist's Role

Pharmacists often see hints of alcoholism, such as poor hepatic function or vitamin deficiencies. But studies have shown that, especially among women, alcohol-use disorders are often overlooked due to inconsistencies in screening, poor screening tools, and lack of staff awareness.[55,56] Pharmacists can improve care by measuring and recording drinking consistently as an "*x* year, *y* drinks per day" habit, like smoking is measured.

In addition, pharmacists should stay abreast of changes in available drug treatments. Until recently, only disulfiram was available to treat alcohol-use disorders. The new agents promise better treatment (see Exhibit 6.5).

EXHIBIT 6.5.
Cutting Edge: Abstinence in a Vial

Ideally, a pharmacological intervention for alcohol dependence or abuse would decrease cravings, block the reinforcement that intoxication delivers, and be free of side effects. Although no such agent is available now, progress is being made.

Acamprosate. Tested in multicenter, placebo-controlled clinical trials with more than 4,500 patients with alcohol dependence, acamprosate consistently increased abstinence rates when used with multidisciplinary psychosocial or behavioral therapies. Its mild side effects include diarrhea. Acamprosate is FDA approved for treatment of alcoholism.

Disulfiram. FDA approved for decades, disulfiram produces a highly unpleasant intolerance to alcohol by blocking oxidation at the acetaldehyde stage, leading to circulating acetaldehyde levels up to ten times higher than normal. Alcohol exposure, even topically, causes flushing, throbbing headache, nausea, vomiting, and respiratory symptoms. Patients must be cognitively intact to use disulfiram. Therapy can cause hepatic dysfunction, and extended use of disulfiram is rare.

Nalmefene. Nalmefene is a newer opioid antagonist with no agonist activity or abuse potential. Compared with naltrexone, it has longer and greater bioavailability, longer half-life, no dose-dependent liver toxicity, and binds more competitively with opioid receptor subtypes that are thought to reinforce drinking. Further studies are underway. As yet, nalmefene lacks FDA approval for this indication.

Naltrexone. Approved in 1995 for alcoholism, naltrexone's mechanism in alcoholism is poorly understood. Naltrexone seems to decrease alcoholics' alcohol intake, but recent large, controlled studies

(continued)

(continued)

have questioned its efficacy in some people. The best candidates are people who have been drinking for less than twenty years, are employed, and have a spouse or a similar social support system.

Sources: Adams WL. Alcohol and the health of again men. *Med Clin North Am.* 1999;83:1195-1211; Klein WC, Jess C. One last pleasure? Alcohol use among elderly people in nursing homes. *Health & Social Work.* 2002;27:193-203; Srisurapanont M, Jurusuraisin N. Opioid antagonists for alcohol dependence. *Cochrane Database Syst Rev.* 2000;3:CD001867.

Alcoholism can be a shadow from a senior's past, a current issue, or a helpful aid to socializing or appetite. Each situation will be unique. On the one hand, clinicians generally assess alcohol history poorly. On the other, when dependence or abuse is a problem, seniors appear to respond well to a supportive, individualized, medically oriented program.[57]

With age comes wisdom . . . sometimes.

The Bum's Rush

- *Rod Colvin, in his book* Prescription Drug Addiction: The Hidden Epidemic *(Omaha, NE, Addicus Books; 2002) offers insight into this pervasive problem and eloquently addresses the syndrome as it occurs in elders.*
- *Cindy R. Mogil's book* Swallowing a Bitter Pill: How Prescription and Over-the-Counter Drug Abuse Is Ruining Lives—My Story *describes how the feeling of peace that prescription drugs promote can lead to addiction. She includes a lengthy list of resources.*

NOTES

1. U.S. Substance Abuse and Mental Health Services Administration. The DASIS Report. Washington, DC: The Administration, May 11, 2004. Available at http://www.oas.samhsa.gov. Accessed October 7, 2004.

2. Holroyd S, Duryee JJ. Substance use disorders in a geriatric psychiatry outpatient clinic: Prevalence and epidemiologic characteristics. *J Nerv Ment Dis.* 1997; 185:627-632.

3. Curtis JR, Geller G, Stokes EJ, Levine DM, Moore RD. Characteristics, diagnosis, and treatment of alcoholism in elderly patients. *J Am Geriatr So.* 1989; 37:310-316.

4. Colvin R. *Prescription drug addiction: The hidden epidemic.* Omaha, NE: Addicus Books; 2002.

5. U.S. Substance Abuse and Mental Health Services Administration. The national household survey on drug abuse. 2003. Available at http://www.DrugAbuse Statistics.samhsa.gov/. Accessed October 7, 2004.

6. Widlitz M, Marin DB. Substance abuse in older adults. An overview. *Geriatrics* 2002;57:29-34.

7. Sullivan MG. Two-item screen flags elderly substance abuse: Focus on effect, not quantify. *Family Practice News* January 1, 2004:30.

8. Gfroerer JC, Penne MA, Pemberton MR, Folsom RE. The aging baby boom cohort and furture prevalence of substance abuse. Office of Applied Studies; 2003. Available at http://www.oas.ssamhsa.gov/aging/chp5.htm. Accessed October 2004.

9. U.S. Department of Health and Human Services. 10th Special Report to the U.S. Congress on Alcohol and Health. Washington, DC: NIH; June 2000. NIH publication No. 00-1583.

10. Adams WL. Alcohol and the health of aging men. *Med Clin North Am.* 1999;83:1195-1211.

11. Johnson J. Alcohol problems in old age: A review of recent epidemiological research. *International Journal of Geriatric Psychiatry* 2000;15:575-581.

12. Schanlaub R. A prescription for abuse. *Law and Order* 2003;51:93-94.

13. Kraman P. Rx for prescription drug abuse. *State News* 2004;47:13-16.

14. Amoako EP, Richardson-Campbell L, Kennedy-Malone L. Self-medication with over-the-counter drugs among elderly adults. *J Gerontol Nurs.* 2003;29:10-15.

15. Sitzman K. Over-the-counter medications—use caution! *AAOHN J.* 2003; 51(12):544.

16. Dabney DA, Hollinger RC. Drugged druggists: The convergence of two criminal career trajectories. *Justice Quarterly* 2002;19:181-213.

17. Good PM, Joranson DE, Kaplan KO, et al. (eds.). *Prescription pain medications: Frequently asked questions and answers for health care professional and law enforcement personnel.* Washington, DC: U.S. Department of Justice Drug Enforcement Agency; 2003. Available at http://www.deadiversion.usdoj.gov/faq/general .htm. Accessed October 2004.

18. Adler G, Greeman M, Rickers S, Kuskowski M. Smoking in nursing homes: conflicts and challenges. *Soc Work Health Care.* 1997;25(4):67-81.

19. American Lung Association. *ALA Research Awards Nationwide 2001-2002.* New York: ALA; 2002. Available at http://www.lungusa.org/research/copd01.html. Accessed March 7, 2002.

20. Watts SA, Noble SL, Smith PO. Disco M. First-line pharmacotherapy for tobacco use and dependence. *J Am Board Fam Pract.* 2002;15:489-497.

21. Ossip-Klein DJ, McIntosh S, Utman C, Burton K, et al. Smokers age 50+: Who gets physician advice to quit? *Prev Med.* 2000;31(4):364-369.

22. Rimer BK, Orleans CT, Keintz MK, Cristinzio S, et al. The older smoker: Status, challenges and opportunities for intervention. *Chest* 1990;97(3):547-553.

23. Age and the role of symptomatology in readiness to quit smoking. *Addict Behav.* 1999;24(1):1-16.

24. HEBS. Tobacco unwrapped: Smoking cessation guidelines for Scotland. Available at http://hebs.scot.nhs.u/tobacco/smokestop/publlications/SmokePubText .cfm?TxtTCode. Accessed March 7, 2002.

25. Orleans CT, Jepson C, Resch N, Rimer BK. Quitting motives and barriers among older smokers: The a986 Adult Tobacco Use Survey revisited. *Cancer* 1994;74(7 Suppl.):2055-2061.

26. Petty TL. COPD: Interventions for smoking cessation and improved ventilatory functioning. *Geriatrics* 2000;55(12):30-39.

27. Hughes JR. Why does smoking so often produce dependence? *Tob Control.* 2001;10(1):62-64.

28. Kviz FJ. Providers' smoking cessation attitudes and practices for older patients. *Behav Med.* 1999;25(2):53-61.

29. U.S. Department of Health and Human Services. Treating Tobacco Use and Dependence. Available at http://www.surgeongeneral.gov/tobacco/systems.htm. Accessed March 22, 2002.

30. British Thoracic Society. BTS guidelines for the management of chronic obstructive pulmonary disease. *Thorax* 1997;52(Suppl 5):S1-28.

31. Maguire CP, Ryan J, Kelly A, O'Neill D, et al. Do patient age and medical condition influence medical advise to stop smoking? *Age Aging* 2000;29(3):264 266.

32. Shiffman S, Pillitteri JL, Burton SL, Rohay JM, et al. Effects of health messages about "light" and "ultra light" cigarettes on beliefs and quitting intent. *Tob Control.* 2001;10(1 Suppl.):I24-32.

33. Fiore MC, Bailey WC, Cohen SJ, et al. Smoking cessation: Clinical practice guideline no. 18. Washington, DC: Agency for Health Care Policy and Research, U.S. Department of Health and Human Services; 2000.

34. Center for Disease Control Tobacco Information and Prevention. How to quit smoking. Atlanta, GA: CDC; 2003. Available at http://www.cdc.gov/nccdphp/ osh/tobacc.htm. Accessed February 12, 2002.

35. Center for Disease Control and Prevention. Receipt of advice to quit smoking in Medicare and managed care. *MMWR* 2001;49(35):797-801.

36. Kleinman L, Messina-Kleinman D. It's never too late to quit. Available at http://www.drkoop.com/wellness/tobacco/articles/lete.html. Accessed February 12, 2002.

37. Saint Vincent catholic Medical Center. Smoking and your health. Available at http://www.svcmc.org/quickcheck/lifestyle/smoking.asp. Accessed February 12, 2002.

38. Connolly MJ. Smoking cessation in old age: Closing the stable door? *Age Aging* 2000;29(3):193-195.

39. Lasser K, Boyd W, Woolhandler S, et al. Smoking and mental illness: A population-based prevalence study. *JAMA* 2000;284:2606-2610.

40. El-Guebaly N, Hodgins D. Schizophrenia and substance abuse. Prevalence issues. *Canadian Journal Psychiatry* 1992;37:704-710.

41. Lyon E. A review of the effects of nicotine on schizophrenia and antipsychotic medications. *Psychiatric Services* 1999;50:1346-1350.

42. Ziedonis D, Kosten T, Glazer W, et al. Nicotine dependence and schizophrenia. *Hospital and Community Psychiatry* 1994;45:204-206.

43. Dursun S, Kutcher S. Smoking, nicotine, and psychiatric disorders: Evidence for therapeutic role, controversies, and implications for future research. *Medical Hypotheses* 1999;52:101-109.

44. American Psychiatric Association. *Diagnostic and Statistical Manual of Mental Disorders,* Fourth Edition, Text Revision (DSM-IV-TR). Washington, DC, APA Press; 2000.

45. Grant BF. Prevalence and correlates of alcohol use and DSM-IV alcohol dependence in the United States: Results of the national longitudinal alcohol epidemiologic survey. *J Stud Alcohol.* 1997;58:464-473.

46. Maher JJ. Exploring alcohol's effect on liver function. *Alcohol Research and Research World* 1997;21:5-12.

47. Klatsky AL. Alcohol and mortality. *Ann Intern Med.* 1992;117:646-654.

48. Romm EB, Giovannucci EL, Willett WC, Colditz GA, et al. Prospective study of alcohol consumption and risk of coronary disease in men. *Lancet* 1991; 338:464-468.

49. Thun MJ, Peto R, Lopez AD, Monaco JH, et al. Alcohol consumption and mortality among middle-aged and elderly U.S. adults. *N Engl J Med.* 1997;337: 1705-1714.

50. Scherr PA, Lacroix AZ, Wallace RB, Berkman L, et al. Light to moderate alcohol consumption and mortality in the elderly. *J Am Geriatr Soc.* 1992;40:651-657.

51. Gaziano JM, Buring JE, Breslow JL, Goldhaber SZ, et al. Moderate alcohol intake, increased levels of high-density lipoprotein and its subfractions, and decreased risk of myocardial infarction. *N Engl J Med.* 1993;329:1829-1834.

52. Suh I, Shaten BJ, Cutler JH, Kuller LH. Alcohol use and mortality from coronary heart disease: The role of high-density lipoprotein cholesterol. The Multiple Risk Factor Intervention Trial Research Group. *Ann Intern Med.* 1992;116:881-887.

53. Pahor M, Guralnik JM, Havlik RJ, Carbonin P, et al. Alcohol consumption and risk of deep venous thrombosis and pulmonary embolism in older persons. *J Am Geriatr Soc.* 1996;44:1030-1037.

54. Obisesan TO, Hirsch R, Kosoko O, Carlson L. Moderate wine consumption is associated with decreased odds of developing age-related macular degeneration in NHANES-1. *J Am Geriatr Soc.* 1998;46:1-7.

55. Klein WC, Jess C. One last pleasure? Alcohol use among elderly people in nursing homes. *Health and Social Work* 2002;27:193-203.

56. Dole EJ, Gupchup GV. A review of the problems associated with screening instruments used for alcohol use disorders in the elderly. *The Consultant Pharmacist* 1999;14:286-293.

57. Oslin DW, Pettinata H, Volpicelli JR. Alcoholism treatment adherence: Older age predicts better adherence and drinking outcomes. *Am J Geriatr Psychiatry.* 2002;10:740-747.

Chapter 7

Elder Abuse

Unlike every other chapter in this book, this chapter does not begin with a joke. There is nothing funny about elder abuse.

American awareness of abusive relationships—child, spouse, and elder abuse—began to peak in the 1960s. Due to a 1978 investigation by the U.S. House of Representatives Subcommittee on Family Violence, elder abuse became a public concern.[1] Since then, researchers have identified many typical patterns of abuse and refined these definitions as necessary. One factor—the rapidly aging population—will contribute to an increasing number of elder abuse cases unless heightened awareness, effective interventions, lucid public policy, and appropriately stiff penalties combine to create an effective prevention plan.

Aging adults involved in abusive relationships often visit pharmacies, alone or perhaps with their abusers. Many states require health care professionals, including pharmacists, to report suspected abuse. This chapter, although short, will help pharmacists understand this problem and their responsibilities when they encounter it.

WHAT IS IT?

Surveys suggest that 3 to 10 percent of elders are abused or neglected.[2] But, as in every other field of study, findings from elder abuse research can be difficult to interpret and compare, because the field's vocabulary is developing and often inconsistent. In addition, states' laws differ on the age at which a person is considered elderly, reporting requirements, and what is considered abuse, as do reporting

Pharmacy Practice in an Aging Society
© 2006 by The Haworth Press, Inc. All rights reserved.
doi:10.1300/5404_07

processes. The National Center on Elder Abuse (NCEA) describes seven categories of elder abuse:[2]

1. *Financial abuse:* Misuse of an elderly person's money or assets for personal gain, including stealing (e.g., cash, Social Security checks, possessions) and coercion (e.g., changing a will, assuming power of attorney).

2. *Miscellaneous abuse:* Violation of personal rights (e.g., failing to respect the aging person's dignity and autonomy), medical abuse, abandonment, and all other types of abuse.

3. *Neglect:* Failure of a caretaker to provide for the senior's basic needs; this is the most common form of elder abuse and is generally of three types:
   a. Physical neglect: failure to provide eyeglasses or dentures, preventive health care, safety precautions, or hygiene.
   b. Emotional neglect: includes failure to provide social stimulation (e.g., leaving an older person alone for extended periods).
   c. Financial neglect: failure to use the resources available to restore health, prevent decline, or maintain the well-being of the aging adult.

4. *Physical abuse:* Acts of violence that cause pain, injury, impairment, or disease, including striking, pushing, force-feeding, and improper use of physical restraints or medication.

5. *Psychological or emotional abuse:* Conduct causing mental anguish; threats, verbal or nonverbal insults, isolation, and humiliation are included here. Some legal definitions require identification of at least ten episodes of this type of behavior within a single year to constitute abuse.

6. *Self-neglect:* Behavior in which seniors compromise their own health and safety, as when an aging adult refuses needed help with activities of daily living. If a patient is deemed competent, ethical questions arise regarding the patient's right of autonomy and the health care provider's role.

7. *Sexual abuse:* Nonconsensual intimate contact or exposure by any person when the patient is incapable of giving consent.

FREQUENCY AND COSTS

Statistics describing elder abuse probably underestimate its reality. Elder abuse occurs among members of all racial, socioeconomic, and religious backgrounds. We tend to think of women as the most common victims of abuse, but numerous studies have found no differences based on gender. Women may suffer greater physical and psychological injury, however.

When compared with people who have not been abused, victims of violence have twice as many physician visits, 2.5 times the outpatient costs, and a diminished sense of well-being.[3] Annually, the United States spends up to $5 billion on medical, police, and court costs related to family violence; this does not include shelter, unemployment, and reduced productivity costs.[4] For elders, the consequences may be particularly dire due to comorbid illnesses and frailty (frailty is described in Chapter 4). Lachs and colleagues determined that community-dwelling elders with a history of being mistreated had an elevated risk of death (odds ratio, 3 to 1) after adjusting for other factors associated with increased mortality in older adults.[5] They also found that almost two-thirds of elderly victims of abuse had been seen in an emergency department at least once within the five years prior to the initial identification of abuse and that these visits frequently resulted in hospital admission.[6]

DETECTING ABUSE

Shame, inability to communicate, poor literacy, and cultural factors are barriers to accurate reporting of abuse. Patients may remain silent for fear of retaliation or abuse escalation. Frequently, economic vulnerability forces victims to remain in terrible situations.[7]

The Joint Commission on Accreditation of Healthcare Organizations requires ambulatory care settings to have a protocol for identification of and intervention in domestic violence.[8] The American Medical Association advises physicians to routinely ask geriatric patients about abuse, even absent signs.[9] Direct, simple, nonjudgmental questioning increases the likelihood of a candid response. Interviewing patients and caregivers together and separately can highlight disparities in their stories and suggest a finding of abuse. In fact, a caregiver's reluctance to allow a capable patient to speak for himself or herself is in itself a sign of abuse.[2]

Pharmacists are generally not trained to conduct interviews that might identify abuse. There is a list of questions that a trained interviewer might use; the questions themselves shed light on what constitutes abuse. Should you suspect abuse, you may be able to gather information using some of these questions, if you proceed cautiously. If the victim describes situations that may constitute abuse, document your findings accurately and objectively. Good record-keeping will add credibility to your story when (or if) you call adult protective services, and you will be able to present the history accurately each time you relate what happened. (Yes, you will be asked to repeat your story.) The following is the list of questions to use:

- Do you ever feel alone?
- Have you been left alone for long periods?
- Is your home safe?
- Is help available when you need assistance?
- Has anyone failed to help you care for yourself when you needed assistance?
- Are you afraid of anyone at home?
- Do you receive routine news or information?
- Do you need things like eyeglasses, hearing aids, or false teeth?
- What happens when you and your caregiver disagree?
- Have you received "the silent treatment"?
- Have you been threatened with punishment, deprivation, or institutionalization?
- Have you been struck, slapped, or kicked?
- Have you been tied down or locked in a room?
- Have you been force-fed?
- Has anyone touched you in a sexual way without permission?
- Is money being stolen from you or used inappropriately?
- Have you been forced to sign a power of attorney, will, or another document against your wishes?
- Have you been forced to make purchases against your wishes?
- Does your caregiver depend on you for financial support?

If abuse is identified, clinicians might ask these follow-up questions:

- Is it an isolated incident?
- How long has the abuse been occurring?

- Why do you think this happens?
- When do you think the next episode will occur?
- Is the abuser present here?
- Is it safe for you to return home?
- What would you like to see happen?
- Have you ever received help for this problem before?[9,10]

Elder abuse mirrors other abusive relationships in that it rarely resolves spontaneously and it tends to escalate over time. There is no specific injury type or pattern common to elderly persons who are abused. Signs and symptoms of elder abuse may be blatant or subtle, and neglect may mimic the signs and symptoms of many common chronic medical conditions in elderly people. Some observations make elder abuse a strong possibility. The following are signs of possible elder abuse:

- multiple injuries in various stages of evolution (i.e., old yellow bruises and new dark bruises)
- unexplained injuries
- treatment delays
- injuries inconsistent with history
- contradictory patient and caregiver explanations
- laboratory findings indicating medication misuse
- bruises, welts, lacerations, rope marks, burns
- venereal disease or genital infections
- dehydration, malnutrition, decubitus ulcers, poor hygiene
- withdrawal, depression, agitation, or infantile behavior
- strained, tense relationships
- belittling behaviors toward a patient[2-13]

WHAT CAUSES ABUSE?

No single answer explains the behavior of either the victim or the perpetrator in an abusive relationship. A number of psychosocial and cultural factors are involved. Precipitating factors seem to fall into four major categories: physical and mental impairment of the patient, caregiver stress, transgenerational violence, and psychopathology in the abuser.[10]

Researchers have postulated that frailty is a risk factor, but studies do not correlate frailty with elder abuse. Impairment, either physical or mental, may decrease seniors' self-defense or escape abilities and increase their vulnerability.

The contribution of caregiver stress in fueling abusive behavior is highly variable. Some caregivers cope well with stressors like patients' incontinence, addictions or abuse, verbal outbursts, or constant questioning. Others feel anger or hostility toward the elderly person, which may culminate in violence.[2]

Abusers of older adults are both women and men, and are apt to be family members. Transgenerational violence appears to be a learned behavior passed from generation to generation. An abused child may later perpetuate the pattern by abusing his own children—and his parent. For several years, adult children were the most common abusers of family members; recently, spouses surpassed adult children as the most common perpetrators of elder abuse.[2] When the older person and the abuser share living quarters, when the victim depends on the abuser, or when the elder is socially isolated, the potential for abuse is greater.[10]

Psychopathology in the abuser (addiction, personality disorders, mental retardation, dementia, and other conditions) can increase the likelihood of elder abuse. Unfortunately, family members with these conditions are often primary caretakers for elderly relatives simply because they are unemployed and available to stay home.

A WORD ABOUT SELF-NEGLECT

Many elders live on the margins of poverty. They have to choose between food and medicine, and pharmacists may suspect elder abuse when financial distress is the real problem. Pharmacists may be able to refer such older patients to programs for the pharmaceutically indigent (see Exhibit 7.1). Some elders may refuse help or evidence embarrassment because they cannot afford medication. Referring the elder to adult protective services is appropriate in these cases also, because the necessary intervention here is increased social service.

Other signs of self-neglect include hoarding, leaving a lit stove unattended, poor hygiene, and dismal housekeeping. If the elder is deemed competent, intervention can be very complicated. Intervention can be a lengthy process and will require multidisciplinary in-

EXHIBIT 7.1.
Pharmaceutical Indigence: What Help Is Available?

From the states: Volunteers in Health Care's Web site (www .volunteersinhealthcare.org) lists state-level pharmacy assistance programs and contact information. The National Conference of State Legislatures (www.ncsl.org/programs/health/drugaid.htm) has a similar online list that features links to several states' Web sites.

From the forty-eight-member Pharmaceutical Research and Manufacturers of American (PhRMA): PhRMA coordinates a patient assistance program for patients of all ages, called HelpingPatients.org (www .helpingpatients.org). Income criteria vary by sponsor and/or agent. In some instances, a family or individual with a household income of $60,000 may qualify for assistance with some of most expensive agents used to prevent organ transplant rejection, cancer, and AIDS.

From volunteer and nonprofit groups: These groups help the patient complete the paperwork necessary to obtain assistance. Most request a small contribution (e.g., $5). Some will refund the fee if assistance is unavailable. Two companies offering this service are the Free Medicine Program (www.freemedicineprogram.com) and The Medicine Program (www.themedicineprogram.com).

And if medication is not the only problem: The National Council on Aging (www.ncoa.org) operates a free online service to seniors, fifty-five and older, that contains more than 1,150 different programs from all fifty states for heating, utilities, health, nutrition, and tax relief benefits. It also lists an average of fifty to seventy pharmacy assistance programs per state. BenefitsCheckUp (www.benefitscheckup.org) asks users to complete a questionnaire focused on eligibility criteria and then generates a list of potential benefits for which they qualify in their geographic area. Two versions of BenefitsCheckUp exist: one for patients/consumers and the far more detailed one for organizations.

volvement (that is, social workers, physicians, nurses, and administrators). The ultimate goal is to provide the aging adult with a more fulfilling and enjoyable life.

The laws in most states require helping professionals, called mandated reporters, to report suspected abuse or neglect. In most states, anyone who reports elder abuse in good faith is exempt from civil or criminal liability as well as any professional disciplinary action. You are making a report in good faith if you are aware of an incident that, to a reasonable observer, appears to be abuse; if you are told of an incident by the victim; or if you have a reasonable basis for suspecting abuse.[2]

As always, call the police or 911 immediately if you suspect an elder is in immediate, life-threatening danger. If the danger is not immediate, relay your concerns to adult protective services, a long-term care ombudsman, or the police. Be ready to give the elder's name, address, contact information, and details about why you are concerned. You may be asked a series of questions about known medical problems (including confusion or memory loss), family or social supports, and what you suspect. You will probably be asked to provide your name, address, and telephone number, but most states will take the report even if you do not identify yourself.[2]

CONCLUSION

Elder abuse takes many forms and is driven by a variety of factors, including the elder's environment, financial situation, extent of dependency, and the personalities of the patient and caregiver. All states consider most physical, sexual, and financial abuses against elders crimes.[1] Clinicians must use thoughtful and compassionate means of intervention when abuse seems likely.

The Bum's Rush

- *The National Center on Elder Abuse (http://www.elderabusecenter. org/default.cfm), funded by the U.S. Administration on Aging, is a gateway to resources on elder abuse, neglect, and exploitation.*
- *Chemical restraint—any drug used for discipline or convenience and not required to treat medical symptoms—is a form of abuse. Pharmacists interested in this topic might read McGillivray and McCabe's "Pharmacological Management of Challenging Behavior of Individuals With Intellectual Disability"* (Res Dev Disabil. 2004;25:523-537).
- *Mystery author P. D. James's* The Children of Men *explores a world wherein human reproduction ceases, and the last child was born in 1995. Set in 2021, the youngest humans are twenty-six and society faces the problems of the old. The infirm are encouraged to commit group suicide and often those with dementia are herded onto barges and set adrift at sea. This book elucidates how trying caregiving can be and the lengths to which people might go in desperation.*

NOTES

1. Madden C. Elder abuse in the United States. *J Clin Forensic Med.* 1995;2:1-8.

2. U.S. National Center on Elder Abuse. State and National Statistics. 2002. Available at http://www.elderabusecenter.org/default.cfm. Accessed November 2004.

3. Berrios D, Grady D. Domestic violence—risk factors and outcomes. *West J Med.* 1991;155:133-135.

4. U.S. National Institute of Justice, Centers for Disease Control and Prevention. Prevalence, incidence, and consequences of violence against women: Findings from the National Violence Against Women Survey. Available at http://www.ncjrs.org/pdffiles/172837.pdf. Accessed February 14, 2003.

5. Lachs MS, Williams CS, O'Brien S, et al. The mortality of elder mistreatment. *JAMA* 1998;280:428-432.

6. Lachs MS, Williams CS, O'Brien S, et al. ED use by older victims of family violence. *Ann Emerg Med.* 1997;30:448-454.

7. Cammer Paris BE. Violence against elderly people. *Mt Sinai J Med.* 1996; 63:97-100.

8. Joint Commissions on the Accreditation of Healthcare Organizations. *JCAHO* Standard PC.3.10 on Victims of Abuse, 2004.

9. American Medical Association. *Diagnostic and treatment guidelines on elder abuse and neglect.* Chicago, IL: AMA; 1992. Available at http://www.amaassn.org/ama1/pub/upload/mm/386/elderabuse.pdf. Accessed November 2004.

10. Krouse LH. *Elder abuse.* Omaha, NE: WEBMD, 2004. Available at http://www.emedicine.com/emerg/topic160.htm. Accessed November 2004.

11. Lachs MS, Pillemer K. Elder abuse. *Lancet* 2004;364:1263-1272.

12. Soler E, Campbell J. Screening for family and intimate partner violence. *Ann Intern Med.* 2004;141:82.

13. Kruger RM, Moon CH. Can you spot the signs of elder mistreatment? *Postgrad Med.* 1999;106:169-178.

Chapter 8

Sexuality

After her grandfather died, Katie, aged thirty, hastened to comfort her ninety-five-year-old grandmother. When she asked how he died, her grandmother replied, "He had a heart attack while we were making love Sunday morning." Horrified, Katie gasped that people verging on 100 years old surely shouldn't be having sex. "Honey," replied Grandma, "Years ago, feeling our advanced age, we figured out that the best time to make love was when the church bells would start to ring. It was just the right rhythm. Nothing too strenuous, simply in on the ding and out on the dong." She wiped away a tear and continued, "He'd still be alive today if that ice cream truck hadn't come along."

Unfortunately, many professionals who care for elders share Katie's stereotypical belief. They may respond to elders' sexual expressions with embarrassment, incredulousness, or verbal recrimination. Though unfortunate, these reactions are understandable given that, dating back to the Middle Ages, Western society has considered elder sexual behavior immoral. But it is time to let go of old stereotypes since research indicates that sexual activity in our later years is normal.

Any reasonable measure of sexual health includes three principal areas: (1) sexual expression without exploitation, oppression, or abuse; (2) absence of sexually transmitted disease; and (3) freedom from reproductive organ disease.

This chapter examines sexuality from these three perspectives and answers some questions you may have (but may be afraid to ask out

Pharmacy Practice in an Aging Society
© 2006 by The Haworth Press, Inc. All rights reserved.
doi:10.1300/5404_08

loud). Sometimes, health care professionals stay clear of discussion of things sexual, finding the topic touchy or offensive. Yet patients often need to discuss issues of a sexual nature, and to be able to listen and respond informatively, pharmacists need appropriate communication skills and a comfort level with certain topics.

EXPRESSION WITHOUT EXPLOITATION

Although the general public believes that elders lose interest in sexual intimacy, an AARP (formerly American Association of Retired Persons) survey of 1,382 men and women aged forty-five and older showed that elders value sexual activity and good relationships into senescence. In fact, 64 percent of men and 68 percent of women who had partners reported a satisfying sexual life. More than 60 percent of these respondents reported engaging in sexual activity once weekly or more. Elders' view of their partners as romantic and/or physically attractive may actually increase over the years.[1]

Sexuality is biologic, affective, cognitive, and motivational.[2] Change any of these factors and sex lives change. When asked about sexual problems, older men have reported erectile dysfunction (ED) most often. Older women have reported diminished sex drive, anorgasmia, and self-consciousness during sex.[3] Women's sex lives end mainly because they lack a partner (although 78 percent of women and 84 percent of men aged forty-five to fifty-nine have sexual partners, only 21 percent of women and 58 percent of men seventy-five and older have partners[1]). Men's sexual activities are more likely to be curtailed by health problems.[4,5] Exhibit 8.1 describes how pharmacists can discuss these topics.

Of the respondents to the AARP survey, 30 percent acknowledged that better health would improve their sex lives.[1] For both sexes, incontinence can interfere with sexual functioning, as can arthritis, diabetes, and hypertension. Pain, reduced stamina, and disinterest are common. Elders with these conditions may have to modify their sexual activity, but these illnesses do not necessarily alter sexual proclivity (see next section).[6]

EXHIBIT 8.1.
Communication: Sex Talk

So how does one go from discussing the last church bulletin across the pharmacy counter with the rosy-cheeked elderly lady who sits behind you in church, to a frank discussion about her lagging libido? Simple! One doesn't. She won't be comfortable, and unless you are well-informed, you'll probably be uncomfortable, too.[a] You'll need to acknowledge in your own mind normal sexual frequency (there is no "normal"), understand that people may be more comfortable talking with pharmacists of their own gender,[b] and ease into the discussion. Often, a good way to start is to discuss very general genitourinary issues,[b] perhaps saying, "Is this oxybutinin working better than the tolteridine did?" Finally, while it would hardly seem to need saying, counsel in an area that permits privacy.

Good: Avoid technical words, but don't go to the extreme and use slang or potentially offensive language. Words like "intimacy" and "sexuality" are easy to understand, whereas "coitus" is not.[c] Identify what is appropriate language before you counsel (and make sure you yourself are comfortable with the terms you'll use). If you introduce new terms, define them or ask, "Are you following me?" Some clinicians feel comfortable taking about "going all the way," or using the baseball field base analogy.[b,d] But make sure to retain professional boundaries; if the patient exhibits growing discomfort or shock, you may have crossed a boundary. While open-ended questions are usually best, when the topic is embarrassing or uncomfortable for the patient, closed questions (those that can be answered "yes" or "no") may help the patient offer information without furthering their discomfort. Once they feel that they have permission to share and that the listener is nonjudgmental, they may be forthcoming.[b,d]

Better: Take your time, listen actively, and allow questions and answers to flow smoothly. Ask, "What has your physician told you so far?" If you receive the same questions from different patients, do some research and have answers, supported by statistics, handy[b]; for example, you might tell a prostatectomy patient, "Restoration of your sexual function can take up to two years, so it's not time to worry yet."

Best: Make no assumptions and, once you receive information, withhold judgment.[a,b] Consider the gay hip replacement patient; at discharge, a nurse slid a folder across the nursing station counter and said, "Read this when you get home." The folder contained diagrams of appropriate sexual positions after hip replacement—all heterosexual. Remember that around 500,000 lesbians and gay men turn fifty every year.[e] They have sexual concerns, too.

Give concrete examples, like "Most doctors say if you can walk two flights of stairs without shortness of breath, you are okay to resume sex-

(continued)

(continued)

ual activity."[d,f,g] For patients who are seriously compromised, stress going slowly. Before you discuss lubricants and other intimacy products, know where they are located in the pharmacy and how they are used. Have pamphlets handy that answer the questions you hear most often (some sources are listed below), and encourage patients to call back if they have questions later.

[a]Penninger JI, Moore SB, Frager SR. After the ostomy: Helping the patient reclaim his sexuality. *RN.* 1985;48:46-50.

[b]McGovern FJ, Appleman LJ, Chabner BA, Lynch TJ, Jr. Sexuality and cancer: Conversation comfort zone. *Oncologist.* 2000;5:336-344.

[c]Sarkadi A, Rosenqvist U. Intimacy and women with type 2 diabetes: An exploratory study using focus group interviews. *Diabetes Educ.* 2003;29: 641-652.

[d]Conine TA, Evans JH. Sexual reactivation of chronically ill and disabled adults. *J Allied Health.* 1982;11:261-270.

[e]Morley JE, Tariq SH. Sexuality and disease. *Clin Geriatr Med.* 2003;19: 563-573.

[f]Szwabo PA. Counseling about sexuality in the older person. *Clin Geriatr Med.* 2003;19:595-604.

[g]Vemireddi NK. Sexual counseling for chronically disabled patients. *Geriatrics.* 1978;33:65-69.

IS THERE SEX AFTER . . .

Myocardial Infarction (MI)

- An older study found that 90 percent of MI patients return to work, but only 40 percent return to sexual intimacy. Not much has changed since 1977: Sex still scares the heart patient.[7]
- Patients who have stable angina, controlled hypertension, and are six weeks out from their MI are considered at low risk for problems induced by sexual activity.[8]
- Cardiac patients may find they have more energy in the morning and may need to use extended foreplay to gauge their response.[7] They should wait until their last meal is digested before starting sexual activity. Consider using the American Heart Association's *Sex and Heart Failure* (available at http://216.185.112.5/presenter.jhtml?identifier=3590) or *Sexual Activity and Heart*

Disease or Stroke (available at http://216.185.112.5/presenter .jhtml?identifier=4714) to educate patients.

Ostomy

- Ostomates (not a play on words, but the actual term people with ostomies use for themselves!) can and do have sex, although abilities vary depending on the surgery's extent. Counselors stress emptying the pouch, using an opaque pouch if possible, and fastening it securely. Men might consider wearing a cummerbund-type garment; women find that crotchless underwear will cover the ostomy but allow intimacy.[9,10] (If you cannot bring yourself to say "crotchless panties" to an elderly female patient, excellent fact sheets for patients are available at the United Ostomy Association's Web site at www.uoa.org/ostomy _faqs.htm).
- Ostamates can generally resume sexual activity when the wound heals and they feel well, but this may take months. If the rectum has been removed, the perineal scar may stay tender for months.[6]
- Partners need to know that the ostomy has no nerve endings and does not hurt.[9]

Stroke and Parkinson's Disease

- Stroke and Parkinson's disease change facial expression, body language, ability to touch, and communication. Hence, sexual activity will be different after a stroke.[7]
- Men who suffer strokes may have difficulty with erections initially. The problem may remain, or improve over months. Morning erections are good indicators of potential improvement.[7]
- Stroke and Parkinson's patients may need to schedule intimacy for the time of day they have the most energy and use pillows to stabilize their positions.
- Order information on the American Stroke Association's Web site at www.strokeassociation.org/presenter.jhtml?identifier=9065. The Parkinson's Disease Foundation's pamphlet *Love, Sex, and Parkinson's* is available at www.pdf.org/AboutPDF/love_sex .cfm.

Chronic Respiratory Disease

- Patients may need to use their bronchodilating inhalers before sexual activity and should continue oxygen if they use it.[8]
- The respiratory patient should assume the less active position (semireclining, on the bottom, side to side, or seated).[8]
- Although counselors recommend stressing good hygiene and grooming (including aftershave and perfume) for patients with other medical problems, scents and personal grooming products are often allergens for the respiratory patient.
- A good handout on sexual relations for the lung patient is available from the Canadian Lung Association at www.lung.ca/copd/management/living/sexuality.html.

Cancer

- Men who have prostate cancer often experience sexual problems from the surgery, radiation, or drugs/biologics. Warn these patients that sexual restoration can take up to two years.[11]
- Women receiving radiation therapy for cervical cancer are likely to develop fibrosis and must use vaginal dilators and lubricants faithfully. Women taking tamoxifen postmastectomy usually (almost always) experience vaginal dryness and discharge.[12]
- Many partners think cancer is contagious; please dispel this myth.[13]
- Excellent fact sheets are available on the National Cancer Institute's Web site at www.nci.nih.gov/cancerinfo/pdq/supportivecare/sexuality/patient, and on the Lion's Australian Prostate Cancer Web site at www.prostatehealth.org.au/v3/images/ sheet_6.htm.

Diabetes

- Not all men who have diabetes develop erectile dysfunction, although many people believe this.[14]
- Women with diabetes have twice the risk of lubrication disturbances, dyspareunia, and decreased libido that women without diabetes do.[14]

- Try the American Diabetes Association's pamphlet *Diabetes and Men's Sexual Health,* available at www.diabetes.org/type-2-diabetes/sex-and-pregnancy/mens-sexual-health.jsp.

Amputation

- Up to 35 percent of amputees experience phantom sensation, and touching healthy areas may trigger pain in the phantom limb.[7]
- Up to three-fourths of amputees report that amputation had restricted their sexual activities to some extent, more so when they were older, unmarried, or had significant feelings of amputation-fostered self-consciousness in intimate situations.[15]
- Every amputation is slightly different. Amputees can resume sexual relations once the surgical site heals, but some amputees (for example those who have had high-level amputation of a leg) may need more help than others. Referral to a gynecologist (for women) or physical therapist is the best bet in such cases.

See Exhibit 8.2 for information of ethical issues related to counselling about sexuality.

EXHIBIT 8.2.
Ethics on the Spot: Reassuring the Elderly Patient

An elderly man comes to the pharmacy to pick up a tadalafil prescription. He underwent a transurethral resection of the prostate (TURP) several months ago, and had a prescription for four sildenifil tablets, but now, his medication is being changed. He asks, "Will this prescription will restore my prowess?" What do you say?

In this case and others like it, you need to fend off that close-ended question. The patient may be looking for a resounding "Yes," but the correct answer falls somewhere between "Your loss of sexual ability is a foregone conclusion" and "There is a drug to fix every problem."[a] Ask questions, and determine what is happening. Suggest that drugs in general work only when behavioral, and sometimes psychological means are added. Be encouraging, but make no promises. Stress that impotence secondary to TURP can take from months to years to resolve.

[a]Penninger JI, Moore SB, Frager SR. After the ostomy: Helping the patient reclaim his sexuality. *RN.* 1985;48:46-50.

CAREGIVER ATTITUDES

In recent years, our understanding of sexual intimacy's importance to elders has been enhanced by empirical research, clinical experience, and greater insight into the interaction of social, psychological, and biological factors. Sexual intimacy beyond reproductive function is crucial to self-concept, interpersonal relationship maintenance, and a sense of integrity. Gerontologists recognize sexual intimacy as a pleasure that can and should linger into advanced age.[16] But what about when elders live in a communal setting?

Clinicians may discourage or be intolerant of sexual expression among elders who live in institutional or supervised situations.[17,18] State and federal regulations (as well as compassion and courtesy) promote residents' privacy as a basic human right, not solely to allow sexual activity or masturbation. In nursing homes, individual rooms are generally unlocked, but staff should knock and ask permission before entering. (Emergent care needs, of course, sometimes supersede privacy needs.)

The issue of nursing home residents' rights is complicated because a majority of residents are physically or mentally challenged. Losses in competency, such as memory loss and impaired judgment, tend to occur gradually. The line between sexual abuse and consensual sex when residents (one or both of whom have dementia) develop sexual relationships also blurs gradually. Therefore, clinicians must judge every situation individually and carefully. Remember that at any age, a person who is financially incompetent, for example, may be emotionally competent.[6,19] (See Chapter 10, "Lost Minds," for more on this subject.)

SEXUALLY TRANSMITTED DISEASES

According to the Centers for Disease Control and Prevention (CDC), sexually transmitted human immunodeficiency virus (HIV), is increasingly common among older people. Since the early 1980s, people older than fifty accounted for about 10 percent of all HIV cases, and the mode of transmission was usually blood transfusion.

In 1996, 11 percent of newly diagnosed AIDS cases occurred in people older than fifty, which does not appear to be a large increase. Now, however, transmission by blood transfusion is rare, and heterosexual contact and IV drug use are the main causes of HIV infection in our seniors. In 2002, people older than fifty comprised 15.9 percent of all new cases of HIV. Heterosexual transmission in men over fifty is up 94 percent and in women 107 percent since 1991. Older Americans remain in denial about their risk for HIV and tend to scoff at the relevance of AIDS prevention campaigns to their own lives. Unfortunately, they are more likely to be diagnosed in the later stages of HIV, and die more quickly.[20] Why? Physicians often ignore the possibility that symptoms may be HIV related, thinking it unlikely, and elders may confuse some of HIV's important symptoms with normal aging.

Many elders lose their partners and resume dating. For them, counseling on sexually transmitted diseases (STDs) is often overlooked, but sorely needed.[2] STDs other than HIV can lay dormant, rearing their ugly heads only years later. Necessary (but not sufficient) for cervical neoplasm, human papillomavirus (HPV) infection, for example, generally occurs early in life, but the odds of developing cervical cancer, which occurs late in life, are 12.2 times greater in women who are positive for HPV. Thus, once infected with HPV, one remains positive for life, and cervical cancer is by extension an STD.[21] Although cervical cancer has a low incidence after age sixty-five and long preclinical interval, it is a serious concern and a nuisance to treat. Women older than sixty-five represent 13 percent of American women, but they account for 25 percent of new cervical cancer cases and 41 percent of cervical cancer deaths.[21]

The rate of false-positive pap smears may be higher in elderly women because atopic cellular changes mimic neoplastic changes. False negatives also occur.[21] Even those women who have had total hysterectomies should have regular pap smears, as the tissues at the vagina's summit are identical to cervical cells, and vaginal cancer can occur. After age sixty-five and three normal annual pap smears, women are safe having pap smears every two to four years.

WOMEN'S REPRODUCTIVE ORGANS

Females of other species ovulate and can reproduce through their old age. Human females' urogenital senescence begins abruptly around the time of menopause, occurring at an average age of fifty-one, with a normal range of forty-five to fifty-five.[22] Among women, age-related estrogen and hormonal changes create actual physical challenges. Vaginal atrophy can cause dyspareunia (painful intercourse) and decrease the frequency of, but not the desire for, sexual contact.

Perimenopausal symptoms depend on several factors, with heredity playing the most prominent role. Smoking, radiation or chemotherapy exposure, vegetarian diet, and malnourishment hasten menopause. Conversely, diets high in meat or alcohol tend to delay menopause.[22] Clinically, surging follicle-stimulating hormone (FSH) levels (greater than 25 to 40 mIU/ml.) usually confirm menopause.

Surgical menopause occurs after total hysterectomy (removal of the ovaries). Partial hysterectomy (removal of the uterus and cervix but not the ovaries) usually prevents premature menopause, although changes in blood flow to the ovaries can cause some symptoms.[23] Pharmacists, because of the drug therapy implications, should be aware that hysterectomy procedures have changed considerably since before 1965, when subtotal hysterectomy (leaving the cervix in place) was common.

After menopause, more than half of women have urogenital problems.[24] Sharing embryological origin, the vagina and urethra respond to similar hormonal stimuli. Vaginitis and recurrent urinary tract infections, urinary frequency, urinary urgency, and dysuria are common.[25]

Traditionally, clinicians have recommended oral hormone replacement therapy (HRT) to treat urogenital symptoms and hot flashes, and to prevent osteoporosis. Women with an intact uterus typically took an estrogen and progesterone regimen to prevent endometrial thickening, which increases endometrial cancer risk. Women whose uterus was surgically removed took estrogen alone. Recently, findings that HRT increases the incidence of cardiac problems have forced clinicians and patients to evaluate the risk-benefit balance of HRT.[23]

Clearly, HRT is contraindicated in women who have vaginal bleeding of unknown cause; a history of breast, endometrial, or uterine cancer; a history of thrombosis; or chronic liver disease. In addition, women should be aware that HRT can cause existing fibroids to grow. On the other hand, HRT markedly decreases calcium loss from bones and reduces osteoporosis risk. Its role in heart disease is still uncertain, although women who have certain cardiac risk factors must clearly avoid HRT.

CDC's workbook *To Be or Not to Be—On Hormone Replacement Therapy: A Workbook to Help You Explore Your Options* is available at http://www.cdc.gov/nccdphp/pdf/HRT_Workbook.pdf. The workbook can help women make informed decisions about HRT, taking into account their beliefs and unique risk factors. Complete and easy to use, the publication presents information in a clear, conversational tone.

If oral HRT is contraindicated, delivering estrogen directly to the urogenital tissue with estrogen creams or inserts is an option. Women, who have had estrogen-sensitive tumors, are sensitive to systemic HRT, or are concerned about the risks of systemic HRT, may find these products suitable. Topical estrogens can relieve urogenital symptoms, but will not alleviate hot flashes or help prevent osteoporosis. Estrogen vaginal creams are generally used daily at first, then three or more times weekly.

The ninety-day estradiol vaginal ring is inserted much like a diaphragm. Women (and their sexual partners) will find the ring comfortable, but it should be removed if infection develops. Side effects include increased vaginal secretion, vaginal itching or discomfort, and/or abdominal pain.[25,26] Like conventional estrogen or first-line lipid lowering agents, the estradiol ring improves lipid profile in women aged sixty years or older.[27,28] Vaginal rings containing both estrogen and progesterone are currently being tested.[29]

Pelvic Organ Prolapse

Up to 41 percent of postmenopausal women experience loss of pelvic cradle muscle tone, including uterine prolapse (the uterus falling into the vagina), cystocele (the bladder slipping into the vagina), or rectocele (the rectum bulging into the vagina). In severe but not unusual cases, tissues from the falling organ may protrude rectally or vaginally. Women may report pelvic cradle heaviness or pressure, abdominal discomfort, bladder outlet obstruction, stress incontinence, and/or urinary frequency.[30]

Studies to determine the causes of prolapse have been inconclusive or marginally indicative. Urinary incontinence, voiding dysfunction, smoker's chronic cough, posthysterectomy complications, fecal incontinence, and difficulty defecating are possible causes. The foremost factor is parity, with prolapse likelihood increasing substantially with one birth, then increasing slightly with each subsequent birth. The likelihood and degree of prolapse increase with age as well. Hispanic women are more likely to experience prolapse than women of other cultures. Prolapse can be corrected surgically, but 33 percent of women who have surgery require repeated surgical intervention.[31]

Vaginal pessaries (ring, donut, cube, inflatable, Gellhorn, etc.) help many women. Depending on prolapse location and size, different pessaries are indicated, with the ring pessary being most effective for cystocele. Incontinence pessaries are also available to compress the urethra against the upper posterior symphysis pubis and elevate the bladder neck. Fitted by trial and error, pessary size does not correlate with vaginal diaphragm size or any other measurement. Most pessaries are silicone, whereas some contain latex; pharmacists should be sure to inquire about latex allergies in the latter case. Once the pessary is inserted, the clinician must check its placement at one week, one month, then every three months. Clinicians must educate patients, who must be fairly independent, about placement and hygiene.[32,33]

Breasts

After menopause, the firm tissue surrounding the now unnecessary milk ducts is replaced with softer, fattier tissue. Preventive screening for breast cancer increases in importance with age, as 45 percent of all breast cancer cases occur in women over sixty-five. In older women, the sensitivity, specificity, and positive predictive value of mammograms improve.[34] Some evidence suggests breast cancer increases among women who have taken HRT for longer than five years.[22] The American Geriatrics Society recommends biennial mammograms for women younger than seventy-five, and mammograms every two to three years with no upper age limit for women with life expectancy greater than four years. (Less than 1 percent of breast cancer cases occur in men.)

MALE MENOPAUSE?

Aging men also face a decline in sexually related function. Decreases in testicular tissue mass, testosterone levels, and sperm cell production; delayed or poorly sustained erection; decreased ejaculatory force; and increased refractory phase following ejaculation are all normal in men over age sixty-five.[35,36]

The concept of "male menopause" was first mentioned in a sixteenth-century Chinese medical text.[37] Experts have long debated its existence, because testosterone levels decline more gradually than estrogen levels do in women. Free testosterone levels decline approximately 1.2 percent annually for men between forty and seventy years,[35] but remain at levels sufficient for normal sexual response.[38]

Researchers have proposed testosterone therapy similar to HRT to reduce risk factors and restore sexual vitality in men. Most accepted replacement therapies for other conditions reverse a harmful process or minimize potential sequelae. Testosterone deficiency's deleterious sequelae are undocumented at this time. Although these therapies remain controversial, replacement with either oral or topical testosterone is used when deficiency is confirmed. Risks associated with testosterone therapy include increased red blood cells, and replacement is contraindicated in men with prostate cancer.[37]

Sexual Dysfunction

Male sexual dysfunction is characterized by decreased libido, ejaculatory disorders, and erectile dysfunction (ED), or a combination of the three.[35] Numerous factors, including physical or psychological stress and, most often, excessive alcohol intake, can lower testosterone levels and contribute to sexual dysfunction.[39,40]

Along with organic factors, psychological problems, such as depression, stress and anxiety, previous sexual trauma, sexual performance anxiety, fear of diseases, sociocultural and religious beliefs, and relationship problems, can affect libido.[41] Excessive alcohol intake negatively affects libido and sexual desire.[42]

Depression is a conundrum when it comes to sexual dysfunction, because one-third of all depressed patients report preexisting sexual dysfunction. Antidepressants, however, may also induce dysfunction. Selective serotonin reuptake inhibitors, for example, adversely affected 1 to 15 percent of patients in clinical trials. Other studies report that antidepressants induce adverse sexual effects in 20.0 percent of all patients and 23.4 percent of men.[42]

Ejaculation problems include premature ejaculation (ejaculation within two minutes of vaginal penetration), retarded ejaculation (failure to ejaculate), and retrograde ejaculation (ejaculate is forced into the bladder).[35]

Erectile Dysfunction

Formerly called impotence and accounting for 80 to 85 percent of all sexual dysfunction complaints,[35] ED has come out of the closet in the past decade. Why? Direct-to-consumer advertising for the several drugs now available to treat this disorder effectively is the main cause. Among men older than forty, 52 percent experience some degree of ED. Incidence of ED increases exponentially from 5 percent at age fifty to more than 50 percent by age eighty.[43]

Elderly men often have questions about ED; pharmacists should know that ED is common and should explain that effective treatments are available. Patients may want to discuss the matter with or without their sexual partner present. The partner's perspective is often enlightening, clarifying issues that may arise with resumption of sexual function. (See Exhibit 8.3 for information on how attitudes about ED have changed.)

Physical and medical conditions associated with ED include general debility, pain, and muscle weakness. Vascular disorders are the leading cause of ED in the elderly because of decreased penile blood flow,[35] but diabetes, multiple sclerosis, alcoholism, drug abuse, and history of heavy smoking also contribute to it.[35,41,42]

Neurologic causes of ED include cerebrovascular accidents and stroke, demyelinating diseases, and spinal cord tumors or trauma.[35]

EXHIBIT 8.3.
Then and Now: Impotence—A Matter of Mind or Body?

Before impotence grew up and became erectile dysfunction (ED), its treatment was relegated to the margins of medicine, addressed more often with remedies than scientifically developed cures. Boar gall, tiger-penis soup, ayurvedic drugs, bee pollen, and the like often helped, probably via a placebo effect. Early in the 1900s, men ordered electrified jockstraps (by mail of course) to allegedly jump-start their less-than-responsive sexual equipment.

Thirty years ago, experts believed ED's etiology was predominately psychological; a comprehensive medical encyclopedia published in 1967 indicated that the great majority of cases of impotence were caused by mental or emotional disturbance, although the authors acknowledged that a few may be caused by medical problems. Today, we know the reverse is true. This home medical reference also indicated that impotence is caused by senility.

Medicine's interest in ED was rudely awakened in 1983 at a Las Vegas medical conference, when Giles Brindley, a fifty-seven-year-old British physician, stepped from behind a lectern, dropped his trousers, and displayed his remarkable drug-induced erection to hundreds of colleagues.

A decade of improved treatments for ED followed. Generally, traditional antihypertensives were injected into the penis (a mood-dampening process for many) and the results were acceptable. Scientists dreamed of an oral medication that could be taken before arousal began. These dreams were answered with the current crop of ED drugs.

[a]Conan N. *Men's health series, part II: Male menopause.* Talk of the Nation. Washington, DC. National Public Radio, October 15, 2002. Available at http://npr.org. Accessed June 2003.

[b]Rothenberg RE. *The New Illustrated Medical Encyclopedia for Home Use.* New York: Abradale Press; 1967.

[c]Stipp D, Whitaker R. The selling of impotence. *Fortune* 1998;136; 114-122. NIM1. Rothenberg RE. *The New Illustrated Medical Encyclopedia for Home Use.* New York: Abradale Press; 1967.

Other potential causes include peripheral nerve damage consequent to TURP, rectal surgery, and diabetic peripheral neuropathy.[35]

The majority of male cancer patients report sexual dysfunction following cancer treatment, and men with prostate cancer frequently report ED. This adverse effect is usually of endocrine origin. Etiologies associated with the endocrine system usually include excess prolactin (idiopathic, or due to hypothyroidism), or low testosterone levels. Unlike other treatment-induced and temporary side effects of cancer, sexual dysfunction continues; it may take years to resolve, or it may be permanent.[42]

Medication use also contributes to ED. The following is a list of drug classes associated with sexual dysfunction:

- adrenergic blockers
- angiotensin-converting enzyme inhibitors
- antidepressants
- antimania medications
- antipsychotic medications
- antiulcer medications
- centrally acting agents
- diuretics
- nonadrenergic vasodilators
- sympathetic nerve blockers[35]

Different drug classes affect different sexual response mechanisms; some affect testosterone levels, others decrease intracavernosal penile pressure. Polypharmacy can cause additive problems. One-quarter of ED cases may be caused by prescription and OTC medications, including antihistamines and decongestants.[35] When medication is the cause, pharmacists can work with prescribers to consider a change in dose or a change in drug, or to determine whether a sexual response may be possible with more time and foreplay.[2]

Medications used to treat ED have attracted unprecedented attention recently, with their manufacturers favoring names that suggest vitality and expunge the stigma previously associated with this disorder.[44] Pfizer's Viagra (sildenafil citrate) connotes force and endurance because it rhymes with Niagra.[45] Levitra (vardenafil hydrochloride), with its "le" from the French article corresponding to "the" and "vitra," suggest life, is similar aurally to "libido."[46] Derived from the French word for sky, ceil, Eli Lilly's recently approved Cialis (tadalafil) implies that the sky is the limit. Furthermore, an advertisement for Cialis adorned a yacht in the America's Cup race,[46,47] Pfizer sponsors a Viagra car on the NASCAR circuit, and the New England Patriots promote Levitra.[47] The success of these marketing strategies is apparent: The stigma of ED is disappearing; even prominent politicians are publicly "fessing up." All of these are effective ED treatments, although they are all contraindicated for men on any form of nitric oxide donor drugs, isosorbide mononitrite, or glyceryl trinitrate for angina.[48]

Prostate Problems

Benign prostatic hyperplasia (BPH), or nonmalignant enlargement of the prostate gland, is the most common disorder affecting male reproductive health. Half of all men in their sixties have signs of BPH and as many as 90 percent are afflicted by their eighties.[49,50] Although associated with aging, BPH's clinical signs appear in up to 10 percent of men as young as thirty.[49]

In BPH, hyperplasia compresses and obstructs the urethra, and posterior hyperplastic growth may obstruct the rectum, causing constipation. Symptoms may include difficulty urinating, incomplete bladder emptying, weak urine stream, urge urinary dribbling, and, rarely, renal failure.[50]

There is no consensus about establishing a threshold of clinical significance for BPH or a point requiring treatment. Symptoms fluctuate over time, making precise guidelines impossible.[49] Common diagnostic tools include a digital rectal examination (DRE), serum prostate-specific antigen (PSA), urinalysis, and creatinine clearance.[50]

Once diagnosed, treatment options for BPH include watchful waiting, pharmacotherapy, and surgery. For men untroubled by symptoms, watchful waiting is prudent. However, refractory retention, recurring urinary tract infections, recurring or persistent hematuria, bladder stones, and renal insufficiency require immediate attention. Generally, TURP or open prostatectomy are surgical options.[49,50] New fiberoptic and laser technologies for prostate tissue reduction offer promise.[49] Pharmacists should know that almost 75 percent of men will have dry ejaculation after TURP. Many patients dislike this condition, but it is not painful and should cause no worry.[11]

Most new BPH cases require more than watchful waiting but do not qualify for surgical intervention. In these instances, pharmacotherapy is warranted. Selective alpha-1 blockers (terosin, doxazocin, tamsulosin) reduce smooth muscle tone at the bladder neck and facilitate urinary flow. Terazosin and doxazosin are indicated both for BPH and its frequent comorbidity, hypertension. Because both agents may cause hypotension, careful titration and close monitoring are necessary. The alpha-1 blockers improve urinary flow, but do not reduce the prostate gland's size.[50]

Because 5-alpha reductase converts testosterone to dihydrotestosterone in the prostate gland, a 5-alpha reductase inhibitor may be used for enlarged prostates. Finasteride (Proscar) is the sole 5-alpha reductase inhibitor approved to date.[50] A three-year follow-up study demonstrated that finasteride reduced prostatic volume by 27 percent and increased urinary flow by 2.3 mL/sec. Approximately 5.0 percent of treated men experience ED, decreased ejaculatory volume, or decreased libido, compared with an incidence of 1.5 percent of placebo-treated men.[49]

Prostate Cancer

Prostate cancer follows only lung cancer as a cancer-related cause of death in men. American men have a 15 percent lifetime risk of prostate cancer and a 3 percent risk of dying from it. More than 75 percent of newly diagnosed cases and 90 percent of prostate cancer deaths occur in men older than sixty-five. Risk and incidence are higher for African-American males.[51] Pharmacists should consider the following facts:

- In 2000, approximately 1.6 million men were diagnosed with prostate cancer.
- Bone metastases are detected in 65 to 75 percent of men with advanced disease.
- In men living with advanced metastatic prostate cancer, who received androgen deprivation therapy for at least twelve months, 38 percent had osteoporosis and up to 50 percent vertebral fractures.[52]

Positive DRE and PSA screening of 4 ng/mL are clinically significant, although PSA testing alone misses 10 to 20 percent of cases. Pharmacists need to know about PSA numbers, because patients do (one urologist told the author, "These old guys carry their numbers around in their wallets."). About 70 percent of cancers detected in PSA screening are organ confined. Biopsy and subsequent surgery are recommended treatments after abnormal PSA findings. Patients undergoing prostatectomy are more likely to have ED (80 percent) and urinary leakage (49 percent).[51] Recently, researchers learned that PSA velocities (increases over time) of greater than 2 ng/ mL in the year prior to diagnosis are significantly associated with mortality.[53]

CONCLUSION

After all this, you may be better informed, but no less willing to discuss these issues with patients. Or any given patient may be uncomfortable discussing sexual matters with you because of your gender or other issues unknown to you. If that is the case, the best thing you can do is refer the patient to another health care professional.

NOTES

1. Walker BL. *Sexuality and the Elderly.* Westport, CT: Greenwood Press; 1997.

2. Szwabo PA. Counseling about sexuality in the older person. *Clin Geriatr Med.* 2003;19:595-604.

3. Clements M. Sex after 65. *The Washington Post Parade Magazine,* March 17, 1996, 4-6.

4. Palmore E. *Social Patterns in Normal Aging: Findings from the Duke Longitudinal Survey.* Durham, NC: Duke University Press;1981.

5. Bachmann GA, Leiblum SR. Sexuality in sexagenarian women. *Maturitis* 1991;13:43-50.

6. Walker BL. *Sex and Sexuality in Long-term Care.* Washington, DC: American Health Care Association; 2000.

7. Conine TA, Evans JH. Sexual reactivation of chronically ill and disabled adults. *J Allied Health* 1982;11:261-270.

8. Vemireddi NK. Sexual counseling for chronically disabled patients. *Geriatrics* 1978;33:65-69.

9. Penninger JI, Moore SB, Frager SR. After the ostomy: Helping the patient reclaim his sexuality. *RN* 1985;48:46-50.

10. United Ostomy Association. Sex and the single ostamate. Available at http://www.uoa.org/ostomy_faqs.htm. Accesed June 4, 2004.

11. Anti-Cancer Foundation of Southern Australia. Prostate cancer: Sexual function after treatment. Available at http://www.prostatehealth.org.au/v3/images/sheet6 .htm. Accessed June 4, 2004.

12. McGovern FJ, Appleman LJ, Chabner BA, Lynch TJ, Jr. Sexuality and cancer: Conversation comfort zone. *Oncologist* 2000;5:336-344.

13. The Cleveland Clinic. Taking time: Support for people with cancer and the people who care about them. Available at http://www.clevelandclinic.org/health/ healthinfo/docs/1100/1184.asp?index_5893. Accessed July 3, 2004.

14. Sarkadi A, Rosenqvist U. Intimacy and women with type 2 diabetes: An exploratory study using focus group interviews. *Diabetes Educ.* 2003;29:641-652.

15. Williamson GM, Walters AS. Perceived impact of limb amputation on sexual activity: A study of adult amputees. 1996. Available at http://www.amputee-online .com/amputee/study1.html. Accessed December 2004.

16. Butler RN, Lewis MI. Myths and realities of sex in the later years. *Provider* 1987;13:11-13.

17. Eliason MJ. Working with lesbian, gay, and bisexual people. Reducing negative stereotypes via inservice education. *J Nurs Staff Dev.* 1996;12:127-132.

18. Haffner D. Sexuality and aging: The family physician's role as educator. *Geriatrics* 1994;49:26.

19. Berger JT. Sexuality and intimacy in the nursing home: A romantic couple of mixed cognitive capacities. *J Clin Ethics* 2000;11:309-313.

20. Centers for Disease Control and Prevention. AIDS/HIV; Number of new AIDS cases, 2002. Available at http://www.cdc.gov/nchs/data/hus/tables/2003/ 03hus053.pdf. Accessed December 2004.

21. Mandelblatt JS, Phillips RN. Cervical cancer: How often and why to screen older women. *Geriatrics* 1996;51:45-48.

22. Healy B. The mysteries of menopause. *U.S. News and World Report.* November 18, 2002:39.

23. Carter L. *To be or not to be—on hormone replacement therapy: A workbook to help you explore your options.* Atlanta, GA: CDC; 2002:33.

24. Milsom I. Rational prescribing for postmenopausal urogenital complaints. *Drugs Aging* 1996;9:78-86.

25. Barentsen R, van de Weijer PH, Schram JH. Continuous low dose estradiol released from a vaginal ring versus estradiol cream for urogenital atrophy. *Eur J Obstet Gynecol Repord Biol.* 1997;71:73-80.

26. Pharmacia, Upjohn Co. *Estring complete prescribing information.* Kalamazoo, MI: The company; 2002.

27. Naessen T, Rodriguez-Macias K. Endometrial thickness and uterine diameter not affected by ultra-low doses of 17beta-estradiol in women. *Am J Obstet Gynecol.* 2002;186:944-947.

28. Naessen T, Rodriguez-Macias K, Litchell H. Serum lipid profile improved by ultra-low doses of 17beta-estradiol in elderly women. *J Clin Endocrine Met.* 2001; 86:2757-2762.

29. Maruo T, Mishell DR, Ben-Chetrit A, Hochner-Celnikier D, et. al. Vaginal rings delivering progesterone and estraidiol may be a new method of hormone replacement therapy. *Fertil Steril.* 2002;78:1010-1016.

30. Romani LJ, Chaikim DC, Blaivas JG. The effect of genital prolapse on voiding. *J Urol.* 1999;161:581-586.

31. Hendrix SL, Clark A, Nygaard I, Aragaki A, et al. Pelvic organ prolapse in the Women's Health Initiative: Gravity and gravidity. *Am J Gynocol.* 2002;186: 1160-1166.

32. Pott-Grinstein E, Newcomer JR. Gynecologists' patterns of prescribing pessaries. *J Reproduct Med.* 2001;46:205-208.

33. Palumbo MV. Pessary placement and management. *Ostomy Wound Care* 2000;46:40-45.

34. Noe CA, Barry PP. Healthy aging: Guidelines for cancer screening and immunizations. *Geriatrics* 1996;51:75-83.

35. Conan N. Men's health series, part II: Male menopause. Washington, DC: Talk of the Nation, National Public Radio; October 15, 2002. Available at http://npr.org. Accessed June 2003.

36. Commentary. Which androgen for the andropause? DHT or testosterone? *Internal Medicine Alert* 2002;24:76.

37. Pope HG, Jr, Cohane GH, Kanayama G, Siegel AJ, Hudson JI. Testosterone gel supplementation for men with refractory depression: A randomized, placebo-controlled trial. *Am J Psychiatry* 2003;160:105-111.

38. Okun MS, Walter BL, McDonald WM, Tenover JL, Green J, Juncos JL, DeLong MR. Beneficial effects of testosterone replacement for the nonmotor symptoms of Parkinson's disease. *Arch Neurol.* 2002;59:1750-1753.

39. Gould DC, Petty R, Jacobs HS. For and against: The male menopause—does it exist? *BMJ* 2000;320:858-861.

40. JAMA patient page. Silence about sexual problems can hurt patients. *JAMA* 1999;281:584.

41. Korenman SG. Epidemiology of erectile dysfunction. *Endocrine* 2004; 23:87-91.

42. U.S. National Institutes of Health. National Cancer Institute. Sexuality and Reproductive issues. October 7, 2001. Available at http:cancer.gov. Accessed June 6, 2003.

43. "Menopause" [A commentary]. *BMJ.* 2000;231:451.

44. As potent as its moniker: Branding medicine. *The Economist* January 18, 2003;65.

45. Kirkwood J. *What's in a name?* San Francisco, CA: Igor Ageing; September 1, 2003. Available at www.igorinternational.com. Accessed October 31, 2003.

46. Gertsel J. What's in a name? Elevated drug sales. *Toronto Star.* August 22, 2003. Available at http://www.thestar.com. Accessed December 20, 2003.

47. Rowland C. Pats ink Levitra marketing deal impotence drugs turning to sports in battle for sales. *Boston Globe.* September 12, 2003:D1.

48. Carrier S. Pharmacology of phosphodiesterase 5 inhibitors. *Can J Urol.* 2003;(10 Suppl.) 1:12-16.

49. Beduschi R, Beduschi MC, Oesterling JE. Benign prostatic hyperplasia: Use of drug therapy in primary care. *Geriatrics* 1998;53:24-40.

50. Chow RD. Benign prostatic hyperplasia. Patient evaluation and relief of obstructive symptoms. *Geriatrics* 2001;56:33-38.

51. U.S. Preventive Services Task Force. Recommendations rationale: Screening for prostate cancer. Bethesda, MD: AHRQ; 2002. Available at http://www.arhq.gov/clinic/3rduspstf/prostatescr/prostaterr.htm. Accessed February 4, 2004.

52. Stanford JL, Feng Z, Hamilton AS, et al. Urinary and sexual function after radical prostatectomy for clinically localized prostate cancer: The prostate cancer outcomes study. *JAMA* 2000;283:354-360.

53. D'Amico AV, Chen MH, Roehl KA, Catalona WJ. Preoperative PSA velocity and the risk of death from prostate cancer after radical prostatectomy. *N Engl J Med.* 2004;351:125-135.

Chapter 9

Stress

From birth to age eighteen, a girl needs good parents;
from eighteen to thirty-five, she needs good looks;
from thirty-five to fifty-five, she needs a good personality;
and from fifty-five on, a girl needs cash.

Sophie Tucker

Old age can be a time of overwhelming and uncontrollable illness and loss.[1] It can also be a time of uncontrollable change. Many people believe that old age is a time of unwelcome but persistent stress associated with decline and isolation. Is this true? Sophie Tucker (1884–1966), the last of Red Hot Mamas, knew in the middle of the twentieth century what scientists and researchers are confirming now. A finely tuned combination of social influences, personality, and financial factors predicts how all seniors (not just "girls") will deal with aging, stress, and the stress of aging.[2] Compared with younger people, how do older adults cope? What do they worry about? How is their experience of stress different?

STRESS, STRESSORS, AND WORRY

For the purposes of this chapter, we will consider stress a state of physiological and/or psychological strain caused by adverse stimuli, physical, mental, or emotional, internal or external, that tend to disturb functioning. Most people naturally desire to avoid states of stress brought on by stressors, although some stressors (eventually) bring joy and happiness. Consider marriage or moving. Marriage at any age

Pharmacy Practice in an Aging Society
© 2006 by The Haworth Press, Inc. All rights reserved.
doi:10.1300/5404_09

is generally a happy affair, although the process of preparation is stressful. For a young adult eager to establish himself, moving is an entirely different experience than it is for a senior who reluctantly downsizes and moves to an assisted living facility. And most of us have had the experience of dreading a change, only to make that change and think, "Why didn't I do this sooner?" (My own grandmother would not even entertain the idea of relocating from almost total isolation in her apartment of decades until a persuasive home-health aide convinced her to do so. Once there, she attended every group event she could and blossomed. Became their top wheelchair bowler for years, actually.)

Stressors come in many shapes and sizes. They can be interpersonal, social, medical or physical, financial, or environmental. The stressors that have the most harmful effects on people's health and sense of wholeness are those that challenge or occur in their most valued roles. Typical valued roles might be associated with work, church membership, family, hobbies, or community involvement. So, losing one's job or being fired is usually more harmful to the psyche and overall health than, say, getting a parking ticket (unless you are a courier by trade, and this parking ticket will lead to license revocation).[3] Harmful kinds of stressors chip away at life's meaning, and cause considerably more worry (uncontrolled negative thoughts and images[4]) than do stressors that arise in less important roles.

Personality

Most people could probably describe their idea of a "good" personality, but scientists have tried to identify specific personality traits and states that usher elders to well-being and longevity. Since 1994, Perls and Silver have followed many centenarians and their siblings, primarily to study dementia. They found that the hypothesis that centenarians have less stress in their lives was wrong. Indeed, they often reported more stressful events than their contemporaries. The difference was that they were more adaptable.[5] Coincidentally, Perls and Silver looked at the psychological traits that may prolong life and found that personality states and traits become especially important when health is threatened.[6]

Before considering personality states and traits, consider personality in general. It is largely stable over time, but it can be variable over situations. That is, aspects or elements of personality may change, temporarily or permanently, in response to changing circumstances. Researchers know that personality is more malleable at life's extremes (childhood and old age).[6]

The following list differentiates between personality *traits* and personality *states:*

Personality Traits		Personality States
Warmth	Suspiciousness	Anxiety
Intelligence	Imagination	Stress
Dominance	Shrewdness	Depression
Enthusiasm	Insecurity	Regression
Extroversion	Radicalism	Fatigue
Conscientiousness	Self-sufficiency	Guilt
Boldness	Self-discipline	Arousal[6]
Sensitivity	Tension	

Personality traits are distinguishing features of an individual's nature that seem to have a genetic component. They tend to be consistent and enduring into old age, although some are more enduring than others. Researchers have found that late in life intelligence, dominance, and conscientiousness tend to diminish in intensity.[6] Personality states relate more to mood, are more transient, and can be affected by a broad array of factors. Regression (a return to earlier thoughts or behavior patterns) tends to increase in later years.[6]

According to Guido R. Zanni, PhD, a former commissioner for mental health services in the District of Columbia,

> A personality trait (or personality style) is a stable and enduring quality that affects how a person perceives, thinks, and reacts. It's core to perception, cognition, and behavior. Personality theorists have long disagreed on the number of inferred traits. For example, some would argue for the inclusion of paranoid, hysterical, impulsive, and obsessive-compulsive traits, separately from dysfunctional neuroses. (personal communication)

Three personality traits seem to be protective against stress and worry, and associated with longevity:

1. Ability to see successful control of past hardships as proof of competence.[2,5]
2. Adaptability to shift efforts and attention from areas where one has little or no control to those where one has more control.[2]
3. The propensity to be slightly suspicious, which may reduce victimization.[6]

People who approach the aging process with rage and trepidation, refusing to reconcile with natural changes, lack an inner sense of the human life cycle. These people adapt poorly. Many people believe that the inevitable decline that accompanies aging is, on its own, a stressor.[2] It does not have to be.

The good news is that, in general, older people tend to worry less than younger people,[1,7,8] and when they do worry, they worry differently. People aged fifty-five to sixty-four tend to worry the most among all age groups as they face the difficulties of middle age.[7] Seniors are less likely to report being annoyed by—or even having—problems.[1] Older adults worry most about health, world issues, and family concerns.[4] Younger worriers fixate on finances, family, and work.

Older nonpathological worriers (seniors who are not diagnosed with depression or anxiety) focus on the present and its issues, not the future.[8] The accumulation of experiences probably inclines people to see things differently; for retired seniors who have experienced more stressful events in life (a loved one's death, spousal discord, separation and divorce, loss/change of employment, and illness or injury), most hassles may seem minor.[1] Their priorities have shifted, and they see things from a much broader context. In addition, they may have fewer valued roles, having left the stress of the workplace behind, and usually having no dependent children.

Often, older adults can see meaning in adversity, and because of their experience, they are more confident they can handle issues as they arise.[5,9] They tend to use more theoretically mature coping mechanisms; for example, replacing hostility and escapism with problem solving. Because they are retired, they often have fewer roles to fulfill, and it is their social role that gives them a sense of purpose.[9] Stress in their social, most salient, role, therefore, can contribute to poor health and erosion of life's meaning. This is why isolation is so damaging. Note, however, that very few centenarians feel lonely or isolated, and most maintain meaningful relationships.[5]

Pathological worriers differ. They report that their worries increase over time, are more morbid, have greater intensity,[4] and are more future focused.[8]

Regardless of longevity and experience, most seniors have difficulty handling certain types of stressors. True trauma, such as terrorist attack, war, or violent loss, causes emotional wounds or shock that can have long-lasting effects.[10] And few people are prepared for the tremendous stress associated with caring for a dying spouse or relative.[2] A recent study examined women who had been the primary caregiver for a biological son or daughter with a serious illness. The researchers measured telomere length (see Exhibit 9.1) and found that as the duration of caregiving increased, the rate of telomere shortening did, too. Oxidative stress increased. On average, these women lost 550 more base pairs in telomere length than did women in the control group. A telomere shortening of this magnitude seems to shorten life in the range of nine to seventeen years.[11]

EXHIBIT 9.1.
Cutting Edge: **Aging and Shortened Telomeres**

Telomeres are regions of highly repetitive DNA at the ends of chromosomes. They act like an aglet (the plastic or metal sheath at the end of a shoelace), and prevent a chromosome from unraveling aimlessly. Each time chromosomes replicate during cell division, telomeres prevent loss of useful genetic information by stopping the DNA polymerase complex several hundred base pairs before a chromosome's end. When cells divide, telomeres are only partially replicated; in other words, they shorten each time a cell divides. Over a year, a normal individual aged fifty or older loses sixty base pairs.[a]

Aging appears to be linked to shortened telomeres, and prematurely shortened telomeres are a hallmark of many aging-related diseases. People with life-shortening dyskeratosis congenita, a progressive bone marrow failure syndrome that causes premature death, have accelerated telomere loss.[b] Individuals over the age of sixty with shorter telomeres in blood DNA seem to have higher mortality rates

(continued)

(continued)

due to heart disease (3.18-fold higher) and infectious disease (8.54-fold higher).[c] A large study compared men who had experienced a myocardial infarction (MI) before age fifty (an event considered premature) with a control group. Age- and sex-adjusted mean telomere length was significantly shorter in the men who had an early MI; their telomere length was comparable to telomere length in controls who were 11.3 years older.[d] Thus, telomere length is a measure of biological age, may dictate mortality, and probably contributes to medical decline.

[a]Epel ES, Blackburn EH, Lin J, et al. Accelerated telomere shortening in response to life stress. *Proc Natl Acad Sci USA*. 2004;101: 17312-17315.

[b]Vulliamy T, Marrone A, Goldman F, et al. The RNA component of telomerase is mutated in autosomal dominant dyskeratosis congenital. *Nature*. 2001;413:432-435.

[c]Cawthon RM, Smith KR, O'Brien E, Sivatchenko A, Kerber RA. Association between telomere length in blood and mortality in people aged 60 years or older. *Lancet*. 2003; 361:393-395.

[d]Brouilette S, Singh RK, Thompson JR, Goodall AH, Samani NJ. White-cell telomere length and risk or premature myocardial infarction. *Arterioscler Thromb Vasc Biol*. 2003;23:842-846.

Pharmacists should be watchful of seniors with histories of depression or anxiety, those who experience personal trauma or regional disaster, and those who assume a caregiving role, whether by choice or by situation.

Disease-Induced and Iatrogenic Anxiety

Certain medical conditions are associated with higher levels of anxiety. Thyroid conditions, diabetes and hypoglycemia, pheochromacytoma, chronic obstructive pulmonary disease and asthma, seizure disorders, central nervous system tumors and traumatic brain injury, stroke, cardiac arrhythmia, and substance abuse can heighten anxiety and cause generalized anxiety disorder.

Numerous medications can also cause anxiety or exacerbate existing anxiety. Bronchodilators, stimulants, and steroids are well-known anxiety inducers. Many drugs, when stopped abruptly or tapered too quickly, cause a withdrawal reaction that includes anxiety. Benzodiazepines, corticosteroids, and antidepressants fall into the latter category. Fortunately, changes in dose or tapering schedules can alleviate anxiety quickly.

Regardless of anxiety's root cause, communicating with anxious individuals is an art. Exhibit 9.2 gives some communication tips.

EXHIBIT 9.2.
Communication: Communicating News
to Anxiety-Stricken Elders

Anxiety can seriously impede communication. People experiencing anxiety often have clouded thought processes; their minds sometimes go blank, or they may not be able to concentrate. Often, they talk too quickly, have difficulty finishing sentences, or have trouble articulating their concerns. Worry can also cause them to seek medical evaluation, ruminate, and seek reassurance repeatedly. When seniors who are not usually anxious become anxious, it can be a clue that they are not verbally expressing some thought or feeling. In addition to the basics of communication covered in Chapter 3, consider these techniques when communicating with an anxious individual:

Prepare by appreciating how anxiety-provoking the situation is to a layperson. Health, pain, money, the possibility that one might not get what one wants . . . all of these things can cause or aggravate anxiety. Dependency of any kind can also be very anxiety provoking. Prepare mentally for all possible responses.

Understand that anxiety can be contagious, and look for a private area in which to talk. Anxious people will communicate better in a quiet place, and sequestering the anxious person keeps others from "catching" the anxiety. Sit down with the person, if possible.

Let the patient direct the conversation initially by voicing his or her concerns. Say something like, "I can see this troubles you. What troubles you most?" Remember to use open-ended questions. Sometimes, the patient will want an intermediary to speak for him or her (see "key informants" in Chapter 3). If the patient starts to highjack the con-

(continued)

(continued)

versation or redefine the issue, gently redirect the conversation by saying, "Let's finish talking about . . ."

Choose your words carefully. Stay away from emotionally laden phrases ("this stupid insurance company" is off-limits; use "your insurer" instead), and watch out for potentially judgmental words like "only" and "just" ("If you had just kept an eye on your receipts, you would have seen that the total was high . . .").

If the news is bad, determine how much the patient knows or suspects. You might say, "Mr. Michaels, what is your understanding of your insurance's cap on prescription coverage—you know, the maximum amount they'll pay in a year?"

Impart information in small amounts, and ensure balance. Saying, "Your insurance company refuses to pay for any more prescriptions because you've exceeded the maximum for the year," can overwhelm the patient. Instead, say, "You may have met your insurance company's limit this year. Is it possible, or have they made a mistake?"

Describe the patient's choices, if there are any. In this example, you might say, "Perhaps you could call the insurer, or you could call your agent (social worker, daughter, or someone else) and ask her to call and find out why they rejected payment." If the patient responds with, "Can't you do it?" explain that the insurance company will not release information to anyone but their employees, the patient, or people the patient authorizes by power of attorney. Help the patient understand what to expect, if you know. Listing the things he or she needs to have when calling the payer (e.g., copies of all their receipts) and suggesting that they put these items in a logical order will give the patient a specific coping mechanism (getting organized). If the particular insurer has a difficult-to-navigate telephone tree, tell the patient this and ask whether someone might help with the call.

Acknowledge your own feelings and limitations. Dealing with an anxiety-ridden patient can be extremely frustrating, and again, the patient's anxiety may be "contagious"; you or others in the proximity, sensing the patient's anxiety, may become frustrated and anxious as well. Sometimes, you will need to step back from the situation, or ask someone else who remains calm to assist. Pharmacists talk about being part of a health care team, and difficult communication is an ideal situation in which to ask the team for help. A nurse, physician, or social worker can help you explain complex matters to a patient.

Empathize with the patient's feelings. It's fine to say, "I can see why you are frustrated," or, "This would drive me to tears, too."

DEPRESSION

Anxiety often goes hand-in-hand with depression.[11,12] Depression is frequently underdiagnosed and undertreated in the elderly. A barrier to its identification and treatment in this group is the myth that depression is a normal consequence of aging. It is not. Depression can stem from or coexist with medical illnesses. Increasingly, experts are realizing that seniors often express their depression as somatic complaints, particularly pain and gastrointestinal disorders.[13] This process, somatization, is especially prone to happen when depression coexists with anxiety.[12]

Depression may be a risk factor for dementia and coronary artery disease. Depression increases disability and mortality, and suicide risk as well. The *Journal of the American Medical Association* published a landmark article elucidating morbidity and mortality issues in 1993. Using the National Institute of Mental Health Diagnostic Interview Schedule for major depressive episode, the researchers evaluated 222 patients who had first-occurrence MI. They followed the patients for six months, identifying depressed patients who were treated with antidepressants for their symptoms and those who were not. Many elders were included and the sample was 78 percent male. Twelve patients died. Depression significantly predicted a fivefold increase in mortality. They concluded:

> Major depression in patients hospitalized following an MI is an independent risk factor for mortality at 6 months. Its impact is at least equivalent to that of left ventricular dysfunction and history of previous MI. Additional study is needed to determine whether treatment of depression can influence post-MI survival and to assess possible underlying mechanisms.[14]

Effective antidepressants are available, but prescribers commonly fail to titrate the dose upward appropriately. Once patients are no longer suicidal or tearful, or begin to brighten, prescribers often maintain the current medication even though the patient has not achieved remission and a therapeutically appropriate dose has not been reached. A depression measurement instrument, such as the Geriatric Depression Scale or HAM-D17, can help quantify response to medication.[15]

Pharmacists can help primary-care clinicians understand this principle by comparing depression scales with quantifiable medical measurements, such as cholesterol levels. Ancillary personnel (including pharmacists) can be trained to administer these instruments. Short of using an instrument, there is virtually no way to measure complete symptom remission.

Clinical progression after diagnosis and treatment of depression can be described using the 5 R's: response, remission, relapse, recovery, and recurrence. After diagnosis and treatment, seniors may improve to remission and/or recovery, or they may relapse at any time. Depression is often a chronic, tenacious illness. The chance of recurrence following a first episode of depression is about 50 percent, increasing to 70 percent after two episodes, and exceeding 90 percent after three distinct episodes.[15]

A common treatment paradigm for any patient with depression starts by treating a first episode for about nine months. (Many psychiatrists will not stop an antidepressant in the winter months, acknowledging a relapse risk for patients prone to developing seasonal affective disorder.) For a second episode of depression, treatment extends from two to three years, and a third (or further) episode reasonably suggests long-term or lifelong treatment. Only complete remission appears to reduce the incidence of suicide.[15]

Too often, nonpharmacological treatments, such as psychotherapy and exercise, are not used as extensively as they should be. Combination therapy is probably more effective. (See Chapter 4, "Exercise and Aging.")

Stress, Depression, Finality

Sometimes, stressors become so overwhelming that seniors contemplate suicide. Approximately 30,000 people in the United States committed suicide in 2002. That placed suicide eleventh on the list of leading causes of death in the United States in 2002, the most recent year for which figures are available.[16] Typically, it is younger adults who commit suicide, but examining suicide in the elderly is chilling.

Approximately 90 percent of unplanned and 60 percent of planned suicide attempts take place within a year of the first suicidal ideation.[17]

Most people who attempt suicide experience an excess of stressful events in the weeks preceding the act.[18] In almost all industrialized nations, men older than seventy-five represent the highest risk group; in the United States, men older than eighty-five have suicide rates five times that of younger people.[19]

Suicide in elders differs from suicide in young people in some riveting ways. In young people, a suicide attempt is more likely to be a cry for help. For example, for every 200 adolescent suicide attempts, one act is successful. In the general population, for every eight to thirty-three attempts, one is successful. One of every four elders who attempts suicide dies.[19] This number is probably low because it does not consider the many nonviolent deaths that are mistakenly classified as natural deaths but are actually suicides.[20]

Elders often plan their suicide far in advance, and carefully. They are less likely to hint at their intent, or perhaps less likely to be heard when they do. Their plans are often detailed and include precautions against discovery.[19] Approximately 60 percent of elders who attempt suicide have a significant degree of illness or disease.[21]

Suicide can be intentional, or it can be subintentional, wherein an individual indirectly or unconsciously causes her or his own death. Men who commit suicide generally use firearms, whereas women prefer poisons, including prescription or over-the-counter medications, or drowning.[22] In the case of subintentional suicide, the casualty may refuse to eat or drink, or fail to adhere to essential treatments.[19] Murder-suicide is increasing and is most often committed by an elderly man who has had to assume a caregiver role for his spouse. He euthanizes his spouse and then takes his own life.[19]

Numerous suicide risk factors have been identified. They include

- alcohol abuse,
- anxiety,
- bereavement,
- cancer, especially newly diagnosed,
- family history of suicide,
- hopelessness,
- intractable pain,
- isolation,
- low cerebrospinal fluid 5-HIAA levels,
- mood disorders, especially depression,

- previous suicide attempts, and
- serious or terminal physical illness, especially heart failure, chronic lung disease, and seizure disorders.[16,18-20,22]

In cases of murder-suicide, a spouse's physical illness and marital discord are the primary risk factors.[19] Strong religious faith and satisfaction with life appear to be protective against suicide.[18]

Recently, questions have arisen concerning the use of antidepressants and the possibility that they may increase risk of suicide. Antidepressants, in fact, can be implicated in some cases of suicide during treatment.[19] Healy and colleagues addressed this issue and proposed five mechanisms by which antidepressant treatment might lead to suicide:

1. By ameliorating psychomotor retardation and enhancing drive more rapidly than the suicidal ideation resolves;
2. By an action intrinsic to the specific antidepressant's effects;
3. By toxicity in overdose;
4. Because of side effects of specific antidepressants, such as akathisia or depersonalization; and
5. Pursuant to treatment inefficacy, either because the dose was inadequate (a common problem) or the specific antidepressant simply did not work for the unique patient.

Christopher Ticknor, MD, associate clinical professor of psychiatry at the University of Texas Health Science Center in San Antonio, says, historically, he described the factors that sometimes lead to suicide after treatment begins as follows:

> Once patients are on antidepressants, their energy levels increase, followed somewhat later by hope. Initially, patients may feel overwhelmed by the things that have happened as a consequence of depression. So, for patients who are hopeless, tearful, have not slept for months, feel desperate, and who are prescribed an antidepressant, it is not the two weeks prior to treatment initiation that represents the greatest chance of self-harm. It is actually the next two weeks, when the patient can mobilize his or her hopelessness and despair and act on it.

Now, however, he says

> Our old paradigm was simply wrong. Until recently, no one had done the research comparing serious suicide attempts in patients before starting antidepressant treatment with serious suicide attempts following the initiation of antidepressant treatment. That research has now been done. In a landmark article appearing in the January 2006 *American Journal of Psychiatry,* researchers led by Dr. Gregory Simon and Dr. Philip Wang studied over 60,000 depressed patients receiving antidepressants over many years. By documenting serious suicide attempts in this population both before and after the initiation of antidepressant treatment, the research team was able to make the following conclusion: Antidepressant medicines dramatically decreased the incidence of serious suicide attempts, even beginning in the first week of treatment.
>
> In fact, the rate of serious suicide attempts was actually four times greater in the week before treatment was started. It should be comforting to clinicians that we can now say with a high degree of certainty that antidepressants statistically save lives, even in the first week of treatment, and do not appear to place patients at greater risk of suicide following the initiation of antidepressant treatment.

CONCLUSION

Anxiety, stress, and depression can be significant issues late in life. They are compounded by isolation and dependence. Dealing with anxious or depressed patients can be emotionally draining. The suicide of a patient, especially when the substance used to commit the act came from your pharmacy, can be shattering and should prompt you to seek help yourself. Understanding the risk factors for suicide is important, as is closely monitoring patients who have histories of anxiety and depression and working with other clinicians to use psychiatric diagnostic instruments.

The Bum's Rush

- *Consider reading any of Irene Marcuse's mystery novels, but especially* Consider the Alternative, *in which several of a geriatric social worker's clients commit suicide inspired by the Hemlock Society's famous guide,* Final Exit.
- *Look at* The Suicide Paradigm *(http://members.tripod.com/~Life Gard/) for excellent information about the processes that result in pain. In particular, educate yourself about penicide—which means the killing of pain. Learning about penicide will help you understand that "wanting to die" has nothing to do with killing oneself and everything to do with overwhelming emotional, spiritual, psychological, or physical pain.*

NOTES

1. Aldwin CM, Sutton KJ, Chiara G, Spiro A 3rd. Age differences in stress, coping, and appraisal: Findings from the Normative Aging Study. *J Gerontol B Psychol Sci Soc Sci.* 1996;51:P179-188.

2. Solomon R. Coping with stress: A physician's guide to mental health in aging. *Geriatrics* 1996;51:46-51.

3. Krause N. Stressors arising in highly valued roles, meaning in life, and the physical health status of older adults. *J Gerontol B Psychol Sci Soc Sci.* 2004; 59:S287-297.

4. Hunt S, Wisocki P, Yanko J. Worry and use of coping strategies among older and younger adults. *J Anxiety Disord* 2003;17:547-560.

5. Perls TT, Silver MH. *Living to 100.* New York: Basic Books; 1999.

6. Martin P, Long MV, Poon LW. Age changes and differences in personality traits and states of the old and very old. *J Gerontol B Psychol Sci Soc Sci.* 2002;57:P144-152.

7. Neikrug SM. Worrying about a frightening old age. *Aging Ment Health.* 2003;7:326-333.

8. Montorio I, Nuevo R, Marquez M, Izal M, Losada A. Characterization of worry according to severity of anxiety in the elderly living in the community. *Aging Ment Health* 2003;7:334-341.

9. Hamarat E, Thompson D, Aysan F, Steele D, Matheny K, Simons C. Age differences in coping resources and satisfaction with life among middle-aged, young-old, and oldest-old adults. *J Genet Psychol.* 2002;163:360-367.

10. Chung MC, Werrett J, Easthope Y, Farmer S. Coping with post-traumatic stress: Young, middle-aged and elderly comparisons. *Int J Geriatr Psychiatry* 2004; 19:333-343.

11. Beekman AT, de Beurs E, van Balkom AJ, Deeg DJ, van Dyck R, van Tilburg W. Anxiety and depression in later life: Co-occurrence and communality of risk factors. *Am J Psychiatry* 2000;157:89-95.

12. Lenze EJ, Mulsant BH, Shear MK, Schulberg HC, Dew MA, Begley AE, Pollock BG, Reynolds CF, III. Comorbid anxiety disorders in depressed elderly patients. *Am J Psychiatry* 2000;157:722-728.

13. Gottfries CG. Is there a difference between elderly and younger patients with regard to the symptomatology and aetiology of depression? *Int Clin Psychopharmacol.* 1998;5(13 Suppl.):S13-18.

14. Frasure-Smith N, Lesperance F, Talajic M. Depression following myocardial infarction: Impact on 6-month survival. *JAMA* 1993;270:1819-1825.

15. Ticknor CB. Pharmacologic considerations in treating depression: A patient-centered approach. *J Manag Care Pharm.* 2004;10(2 Suppl.):S8-15.

16. U.S. Centers for Disease Control and Prevention. *Deaths, percent of total deaths and death rates for the 15 leading causes of death in 5-year age groups by race and sex.* Washington, DC: CDS;2001. Available at http://www.cdc.gov/nchs/data/dvs/LCWK1_2001.pdf. Accessed November 11, 2004.

17. Smith MT, Edwards RR, Robinson RC, Dworkin RH. Suicidal ideation, plans, and attempts in chronic pain patients: Factors associated with increased risk. *Pain* 2004;111:201-208.

18. O'Connell H, Chin AV, Cunningham C, Lawlor BA. Recent developments: Suicide in older people. *BMJ* 2004;329:895-899.

19. Szanto K, Gildengers A, Mulsant BH, Brown G, Alexopoulos GS, Reynolds CF, III. Identification of suicidal ideation and prevention of suicidal behaviour in the elderly. *Drugs Aging* 2002;19:11-24.

20. Juurlink DN, Herrmann N, Szalai JP, Kopp A, Redelmeier DA. Medical illness sand the risk of suicide in the elderly. *Arch Intern Med.* 2004;164:1179-1184.

21. Benson RA, Brodie DC. Suicide by overdoses of medicines among the aged. *J Am Geriatr Soc.* 1975;23:304-308.

22. Hem E, Loge JH, Haldorsen T, Ekeberg O. Suicide risk in cancer patients from 1960 to 1999. *J Clin Oncol.* 2004;22:4209-4216.

Chapter 10

Lost Minds

Three elderly ladies were playing cards, as they had been doing weekly for years. Shirley said, "You know, I'm getting really forgetful. This morning, I was standing at the top of the stairs, and I couldn't remember whether I had just come up or was about to go down."

Elizabeth said, "Ha. The other day, I was standing in front of the open refrigerator, and I couldn't remember if I was putting something in or taking something out!"

Ruth, the hostess, smiled smugly. "Well, my memory's just perfect, knock on wood!" She rapped the table. Then, with a startled look on her face, she said, "Excuse me. Let me get the door."

It happens. Some older folks start to decline cognitively. What is normal ("I can't think of her name—it's on the tip of my tongue . . ."), and what is indicative of serious trouble (forgetting how to maintain and balance a checkbook)? We toss the word "cognition" around every day, but do we really know what it means?

"Cognition" comes from the Latin word *cognitus* (to become acquainted or to know), but like intelligence or emotion, cognition is an umbrella concept. If intelligence is depth and emotion is perspective, cognition is ability. It includes *all* psychological and sensory processes and components that transform, reduce, store, recover, synthesize, and use sensory information. The following is a list of components of cognition:

- Attention
- Decision making
- Language

Pharmacy Practice in an Aging Society
© 2006 by The Haworth Press, Inc. All rights reserved.
doi:10.1300/5404_10

- Memory
- Mental imagery
- Pattern recognition
- Problem solving
- Reading
- Reasoning
- Sensory perception
- Storing and retrieving information
- Writing[1]

Each individual's extensive, multidimensional cognitive processes and abilities combine to form a secret self hidden to others; health care providers must infer mental status from a senior's behavior. Pharmacists who serve elders need to understand normal cognition, age-related changes, memory, higher-order thinking, the distinction between delirium and dementia, and drug-induced cognitive impairment.

Since the 1950s, researchers have accepted that cognition is an *active* (not passive), remarkably efficient constructive thought process of building, combining, categorizing, and transforming information at four stages: sensory input, encoding, storing, and retrieving. Consider that an experienced driver simultaneously converses with a passenger, recognizes and reacts decisively to traffic signals, judges speed while accelerating and braking accordingly, processes information seen in the rear and side mirrors, and mentally maps directions. This everyday, but remarkably complex, set of behaviors shows how efficient the cognitive process is. A new driver's experience is, of course, entirely different. Without memory, discrimination, and other cognitive tools, the roads would be a horror show of perpetually "new" drivers.

Psychologists once thought specific cognitive abilities were localized in separate areas of the brain. From extensive studies of brain-injured patients, we now know that some areas of the brain can assume functions previously controlled by damaged areas.[2,3] The motor cortex is particularly plastic in this regard. Age-related brain atrophy (neural loss) does not correlate with memory loss. Cognition is affected more by acetylcholine levels and hippocampus atrophy than by general neural loss.[2]

MEMORY

Memory has always been a captivating puzzle to researchers. Early evidence supported the existence of primarily two distinct memory types: short-term and long-term. (A third type of memory, sensory memory, buffers stimuli received through the senses; visual, echoic, and haptic mechanisms buffer visual, aural, and touch stimuli, respectively. Sensory memory filters stimuli, allowing only those of immediate interest.)

Short-term (immediate or working memory) refers to the amount of information a person can synthesize and remember in the present (that is, ten to thirty seconds), such as listening to a telephone number and dialing it immediately. Short-term memory's capacity is limited. Humans retain a mean of only 7 ± 2 information items (discrete information bits) simultaneously.[4] To maximize short-term memory, people group pieces of information, consciously or unconsciously, into one item (a process called "chunking"). So, most people process ten-digit telephone numbers by chunking the area code as a single information item. Likewise, readers process whole words or phrases as single- information chunks.[2,5]

Long-term memory is probably of unlimited capacity. Unlike short-term memories, long-term memories are not necessarily sequential. Rather, the brain uses themes or schemata to organize the processes of memory storage and retrieval. These mental "file folders" are constructed, arranged, and accessed differently in each individual, but they probably involve some time connections. That explains why hearing an old song floods people with contemporaneous memories of their first job, old friends, or past events. Forgetfulness is more a retrieval problem than a file deletion issue. Once encoded into long-term memory, memory is probably permanent (but see Exhibit 10.1).

Short-term memory is the entry portal to long-term memory. Without it, nothing transfers to long-term memory. Faulty short-term memory seriously handicaps people's ability to deal with the immediate present; for example, they cannot dial a phone number, or may forget whether they ate dinner. Loss of short-term memory generally can be described as "last in-first out." In other words, the last information bits perceived are the first to be forgotten. Thus, people with early-to-moderate Alzheimer's disease remember distant events but

EXHIBIT 10.1.
Cutting Edge Meets *Ethics on the Spot:*
Wanting to Forget

Forgetful elders cling to diminishing memories, and their sympathetic families seek interventions that would help their loved ones retain this hallmark of their identity. But others who suffer from posttraumatic stress disorder (PTSD) or emotional trauma wish they could simply forget certain past stressful events. Emotionally charged events create indelible memories that can interfere with activities of daily living (ADL). When a memory is being stored, joy, sadness, terror, and surprise flood the amygdala with stress hormones released by the adrenal glands, particularly adrenaline. Adrenaline thereby pairs an intense memory with the "fight or flight" response.

Therapeutic forgetting is the ability to erase painful or recurring intrusive thoughts. In humans, propranolol impairs the consolidation of declarative memory the aspect of memory that stores facts and events by pairing the stimulus and the correct response. Based on propranolol's ability to blunt adrenaline's effect, researchers designed small studies to see whether it can blunt or erase painful memories. Preliminary study results suggest drugs, if taken immediately after an emotionally charged event, may prevent traumatic memories from being stored with disturbing intensity. Additional studies are underway to determine whether drugs may also erase or ameliorate older, embedded memories.

But would the ability to selectively forget alter the essence of personality irrevocably? Drugs that suppress painful memories may disconnect people from the reality or their true selves, or cause historical information to be lost. This poses a complicated ethical dilemma for physicians, and patients and their families. Further, it is unclear whether interfering with normal recovery processes may have long-lasting or injurious effects.

Sources: Debiec J, Ledoux JE. Disruption of reconsolidation but not consolidation of auditory fear conditioning by noradrenergic blockade in the amygdale. *Neuroscience.* 2004;129:267-272; Miller G. Forgetting and remembering. Learning to forget. *Science.* 2004;304:34-36; Vaiva G, Ducrocq F, Jezequel K, Averland B, Lestavel P, Brunet A, Marmar CR. Immediate treatment with propranolol decreases posttraumatic stress disorder two months after trauma. *Biol Psychiatry.* 2003;54:947-949; Taylor F, Cahill L. Propranolol for reemergent posttraumatic stress disorder following an event of retraumatization: A case study. *J Trauma Stress.* 2002;15:433-437; Pitman RK, Sanders KM, Zusman RM, et al. Pilot study of secondary prevention of posttraumatic stress disorder with propranolol. *Biol Psychiatry.* 2002;51:189-192; Reist C, Duffy JG, Fujimoto K, Cahill L. Beta-adrenergic blockade and emotional memory in PTSD. *Int J Neuropsychopharmacol.* 2001;4:377-383; Finestone DH, Manly DT. Dissociation precipitated by propranolol. *Psychosomatics.* 1994;35:83-87.

forget recent information. In many neurodegenerative disorders, short-term memory deficits predict serious cognitive impairment down the road.

METACOGNITION

Metacognition, or what the ancient Greeks called the mind's eye, is an individual's conscious monitoring and evaluation of his or her own mental acuity. Also referred to as higher-order thinking, executive cognitive function, and self-consciousness, metacognition includes anticipating needs, planning, setting priorities, directing changes, and the self-evaluation of cognitive skills.[6] It is metacognition that prompts people to make statements like, "I don't know very much about medicine," or "Sometimes, my mind wanders."

Metacognitive functions are usually remarkably stable and unaffected by age, unless illness and pathology intercede. Frontal lobe injuries and degenerative brain disorders are primary causes of impaired executive cognitive function. (Executive function directs behavior using inhibition, planning, time perception, internal ordering, working memory, self-monitoring, verbal self-regulation, motor control, regulation of emotion, and motivation.) Many individuals with frontal lobe injuries retain specific skills; they lack executive function and are unable to combine specific skills into meaningful goal-directed behavior.[7]

In degenerative disorders, both individual skills and higher-order thinking decline. Often, in the early stages of decline, the executive function recognizes that something is awry. Patients may say or think, "I know the word I'm looking for, but I just can't find it," or "This is my church, but I must have been on automatic pilot because I was actually going to the grocery store next door." Similarly, when the self-perceiving metacognitive function recognizes that deficits are occurring, it may prompt patients to hide their deficits. Remarkably, patients are able to maintain a veneer of normalcy, often for months or years. This common subterfuge delays diagnosis and treatment. Families may also report a quick onset of troublesome behaviors, when in actuality the process has been long-standing.

DISPELLING MYTHS

During the past twenty years, convincing studies have demon-strated that major cognitive decline is not part of normal aging. In a hallmark study, researchers followed 6,000 community-dwelling se-niors sixty-five years and older for ten years. Of the participants, 70 percent showed no cognitive decline after the researchers controlled for numerous variables. Cognitive decline was most strongly associ-ated with atherosclerosis or diabetes and the Alzheimer's-associated Apo4E gene. In people who had two or three of these, the risk of cog-nitive decline was eight times that for those without the disease/gene combination.[8]

Although precipitous cognitive decline is abnormal, several age-related cognitive changes are considered normal. Most involve time (reaction times and performance on timed tests of information-pro-cessing), not comprehension. Language and verbal skills remain surprisingly stable throughout life.[9] Consider the following facts:

- Older adults stumble to verbalize familiar names and words (for example, tip-of-the-tongue experience) more than younger adults do. Watch for this subtle difference: elders use more pro-nouns, possibly because they recall proper names slowly.[9]
- Older adults retain their ability to grasp new material, although memorizing it may take longer.[10,11]
- Seniors have more difficulty multitasking.[12]
- Age slows information processing (e.g., older people complete problems more slowly, but with undiminished accuracy).[10,11]

In addition to slower processing, elders have trouble filtering intru-sive information from short-term memory. For example, seniors have more difficulty than younger people reading text containing words of varying font size.[9] Pharmacists, regardless of age, can experience this problem by reading Exhibit 10.2, which illustrates the subjective ex-perience of eliminating irrelevant and conflicting information. Elders process visual cues more slowly, need more light to read and perform other visual tasks, have less ability to track moving objects, and ex-perience impaired visual search (ability to discern objects in visual clutter).[13] To summarize, the time to memorize information or com-

EXHIBIT 10.2. The Stroop Effect

What does cognitive impairment feel like? Even cognitively intact people may struggle with simple, well-known information when recognition is bombarded with intrusive, but irrelevant information. By experiencing the Stroop effect (propensity to slower performance if, when asked to name a font color, the words themselves are the names of other colors), cognitively intact people can experience what cognitive impairment feels like. Try quickly naming the colors, or in this case, the three shades (**black, gray, and**) of the fonts in each column.

LDJFSL	GRAY
LSJFDL	BLACK
FOCKDC	WHITE
JDOSEX	BLACK
MBSKSY	GRAY
KSISEN	GRAY
SERTLD	WHITE
DKSLRE	BLACK
SLDKFG	BLACK
SLKFOI	GRAY

Naming the colors in the right column is difficult because the automatic cognitive process of word recognition introduces distracting information.

Better examples of the Stroop effect, which use color text, can be found on the Internet. The following two Web sites provide such examples:

- www.apa.org/science/stroop.html
- en.wikipedia.org/wiki/Stroop_effect

plete tasks increases with age. Comprehension remains steady. Highly variable, cognitive decline becomes evident after age 70.[2,3]

MILD COGNITIVE IMPAIRMENT

Research indicates that 17 to 34 percent of elders exhibit mild cognitive deficits that fall between normal functioning and degenerative disorders.[14] Because research has used different criteria for defining mild cognitive impairment (MCI), population estimates are unreliable. In everyday language, MCI manifests as frequent forgetfulness, many tip-of-the-tongue experiences, and frequent "senior moments." Some suggest that up to 13 percent of all elders have MCI. MCI may predict or signal the clinical onset of neuropathological disorders. Studies suggest that 40 percent of individuals suffering from MCI develop Alzheimer's disease within three years.[15]

DELIRIUM VERSUS DEMENTIA

Numerous distinctions differentiate delirium and dementia (see Table 10.1). People close to a senior will describe changes associated with delirium as abrupt and extreme. "Yesterday, she was fine, grocery shopping and paying her bills. Today, she's babbling." Individuals with delirium fail to complete the simplest of cognitive tests (e.g., naming the days of the week backward). Delirium is generally re-

TABLE 10.1. Distinguishing Features of Delirium and Dementia

Feature	Delirium	Dementia
Onset	Acute, abrupt onset	Insidious and gradual
Symptom	Symtpoms fluctuate, worsening at night	Symptoms are consistent
Duration	Hours to weeks	Progressive and continuous
Attention span	Impaired	Normal in early stages
Orientation	Disoriented to environment and cues	Normal in early stages, impaired in moderate and severe stages
Short-term memory	Severe impairment	Slow decline
Testing	Difficult, patient often unable to participate	Patient usually cooperative, and in early stages may try to hide cognitive impairments

Source: Lisi DM. Definition of drug-induced cognitive impairment in the elderly. Medscape Pharmacotherapy 2000; 2. Available at www.medscape.com. Accessed January 15, 2004.

versible and is associated with several common conditions, including the following:

- chronic obstructive pulmonary disease
- congestive heart failure
- dehydration
- diabetes
- medication
- medication withdrawal
- pneumonia
- upper respiratory infection
- urinary tract infection
- recent surgery

Dementia, be it Alzheimer's disease (which accounts for approximately 70 percent of dementia cases and develops from structural changes in the brain) or vascular dementia (which accounts for approximately 15 percent of dementia cases and develops pursuant to vascular diseases like hypertension and stroke), occurs more gradually, developing over a period of months and years. Short-term memory suffers first. Initially normal, long-term memory fades with disease progression, and the patient's ADLs become gradually less attentive and less appropriate. Delirium can occur concomitantly with dementia. Up to 22 percent of ambulatory demented elders experience delirium.[16] (Patients with vascular dementia typically have memory disturbances that are less severe than in AD, such as forgetfulness or problems with spontaneous recall, and that improve with clues and prompting. Language and verbal fluency are usually unaffected.[17])

ASSESSMENT

Because general information and vocabulary are particularly resistant to deterioration,[18] assessment focuses on abilities requiring a high level of fluid processing. Abstract reasoning, spatial perception, and problem solving tend to deteriorate more quickly. Many psychologists use the Block Design Scale of the Wechsler Intelligence Scales to assess early cognitive deterioration. They present a picture depicting a color pattern and a set of multicolored blocks and ask the patient to replicate the pattern with the blocks. While appearing simple, this task requires the ability to understand the whole pattern, break it down into individual units, and reconstruct it using three-dimensional objects.

The Digit Span Test asks individuals to remember a numbered sequence and recite it both backward and forward. This test can identify early deterioration, because it requires attention, concentration, mental imagery, and an intact short-term memory. Digit backward scores that are significantly lower than digit forward scores indicate an inability to maintain visual images and often signal deterioration of higher-order thinking skills.[18]

The Mini-Mental State Examination (MMSE) is another quick assessment tool (it can be completed in seven to ten minutes) used frequently by researchers and clinicians. Its ten questions and thirty possible points assess cognitive skills, including memory, mental imagery, and higher-order thinking. Increasingly, pharmacists are learning how to administer this exam. The following sample questions are from the MMSE:

> Spell the word "world" backwards.
> Can you say "no ifs, ands, or buts?"[19]

The MMSE is sensitive to educational and age bias, so its results must be interpreted with caution. A comprehensive MMSE assesses numerous cognitive processes, including paraphasia (making up substitute expressions), which is a hallmark of Alzheimer's disease. For example, a patient with Alzheimer's who is struggling to name a pencil might confidently say, "It's a soft-writer," or call a key a "lock turner."

Assessing and diagnosing early-stage degenerative disorders require considerable skill. Depression, for example, mimics many symptoms of dementia, and assessment must distinguish dementia from depression-related cognitive decline. Patients must be put at ease, and questioning must be gentle. See Exhibit 10.3 for an example of how the findings of the MMSE can be used.

Frustrated attempts to communicate with cognitively impaired elders can lead to aggression.[20] This is the most common behavioral reason for admission into a nursing home. Health care practitioners in these institutions search for effective behavioral and drug interventions, and direct care staff can quickly become exhausted or scared of the patient.

EXHIBIT 10.3.
Ethics on the Spot: Speaking of Driving . . .

When seniors' driving skills are questionable, a diagnosis of dementia presents an ethical dilemma. Patients in the earliest stages of dementia can drive safely, but over time, dementia decreases spatial orientation, slows visual searching, and causes easy distractability.[a] Each patient, of course, will be different.[b,c] Although it needs to be confirmed by additional research, one model based on postcrash review data suggests that using the Mini-Mental State Exam (MMSE) can help; an MMSE score of 19.9 is associated with an eightfold increase in crash risk. Patients with an MMSE score of 19 to 25 should be referred to the local motor vehicle administration for driving evaluation, with biannual retesting. Those with MMSE scores below 19 should stop driving.[c,d] Other issues—medication use, medical problems, and addictions—also may cause families and health care practitioners to question an elder's ability to drive.

Transforming an on-the-go elder to passenger-only status is heartbreaking. Government agencies responsible for road safety attempt to protect the public from elders with diminishing skill while allowing the invisible majority of older people with good skills to stay on the road.[e] Driving is an economic and social building block,[f] especially in areas with little mass transit.[a] License revocation or surrender effectually disables seniors. Subsequent depression and isolation are common.[a]

What to Do?

Interventions can occur at four levels: the senior, the authorities, the family, or the clinician.

Elders who realize that their driving is declining or might decline can avail themselves of numerous courses. Among the most popular are the Mature Operator Course from American Automobile Association, and 55 Alive from AARP. The State of Pennsylvania's booklet *Talking with Older Drivers* is a wonderful source of information.[g]

It is best if elders themselves decide whether to continue, modify, or stop driving. Sometimes, a change in habits is sufficient to keep them on the road safely.[h] Seniors must also keep their vehicles in good condition and know their car's features and limitations.

The state's main concern is identifying at-risk drivers, rehabilitating them if possible, and making alternative transportation available. Some states have mandatory testing requirements after a set age, and offer graduated licenses (e.g., restricting driving to daylight hours).[g]

Families usually struggle with this issue. Concerned people should discuss potential dangers and alternatives with the affected driver. Taking away an important privilege such as driving without offering alternatives will fail.[a,h] Negotiating limits is a good idea, perhaps

(continued)

(continued)

- agreeing that the elder will drive on only dry, clear days,
- selecting routes that minimize more dangerous left turns (that is, coaching on better, right-turn-dependent routes),[a,h] or
- discussing consequences of driving, including the fact that the driver's insurer may not cover accidents after a diagnosis of dementia or a recent seizure.[c,f]

If all else fails, family members can report the problem to the authorities in confidence.[g] Note that hiding the keys and other tricks are not included on this list. These tactics erode trust.[b,g]

No Thoroughfare

When patients refuse to modify their driving, physicians and other clinicians ought to judge patients' driving abilities, but often have no idea how to do it.[b,h] Occupational therapists are trained to suggest vehicle modifications, exercises, or helping tools that improve driving.[a] Pharmacists can review the medication profile and look for drugs or problems that, if corrected, would improve executive function. Patients on opioids and sedating antidepressants should be told that they cannot drive for five days after therapy initiation or change; if they feel sedated or somnambulant; or if they drink, use illicit drugs, or take over-the-counter antihistamines while on the medication. When necessary and appropriate, the physician must tell the patient to stop driving and send a letter to the authorities.[b]

[a]Johnson EE. Transportation mobility and older drivers. *J Gerontol Nurs.* 2003;29:34-41.

[b]Post SG. Key issues in the ethics of dementia care. *Neurol Clin.* 2000;18:1011-1022.

[c]Nuthall A, Anthony P. Road safety and the driver with dementia: Shifting the debate up a gear. *Nurs Older People.* 2003;15:18-21.

[d]Dubinsky RM, Stein AC, Lyons K. Practice parameter: Risk of driving and Alzheimer's disease (an evidence-based review). Report of the quality standards committee of the American Academy of Neurology. *Neurology* 2000;54:2205-2211.

[e]Dulisse B. Older drivers and risk to other road users. *Accid Anal Prev.* 1997;29(5):573-582.

[f]Krauss GL, Krumholz A, Carter RC, et al. Risk factors for seizure-related motor vehicle crashes in patients with epilepsy. *Neurology* 1999; 52:1324-1329.

[g]Pennsylvania Driver & Vehicle Services. *Pennsylvania's Mature Driver's Task Force: Talking with Older Drivers.* Available at http://www.dmv.state.pa.us/pdotforms/misc/Pub_345.pdf>. Accessed May 20, 2004.

[h]Daigneault G, Joly P, Frigon JY. Executive functions in the evaluation of accident risk of older drivers. *J Clin Exp Neuropsychol.* 2002; 24:221-238.

Aggression in the elderly is an interesting interplay of neurobiologic, cognitive, and environmental factors.[21] Care planning should begin with the question, "Is there a diagnosis associated with this aggression?"[20,21] Logging the elder's aggressive behavior patterns in a diary makes it easier to explore environmental (sometimes called event-related) or biological (nonevent-related) factors.[22,23] Things that annoy or frustrate cognitively impaired elders are often similar to those that annoy cognitively intact people: temperature, noise, light, unresolved familial issues, or specific individuals who grate on their nerves. Unable to verbalize discomfort, they may lash out as their frustration grows. Several rating instruments are available to document violent and aggressive behavior, including the Rating Scale for Aggressive Behaviour in the Elderly, the Cohen-Mansfield Agitation Inventory, and the Brief Agitation Rating Scale.[23,24]

Biologically based violence or aggression can be provoked by unusual, unreasonable, or no stimuli; is often precipitous, escalating and de-escalating with remarkable speed; and tends to be explosive and uncontrolled. Because patients rarely understand the outburst's origin, they express genuine, profound remorse.[23]

When behaviors are unresponsive to environmental interventions or "time-outs," or become dangerous to self or others, medications can sometimes help. The Treatment of Agitation in Older Persons with Dementia Expert Consensus Guideline (available in its entirety at www.psychguides.com/gl-treatment_of_agitation_in_dementia .html) reviews medications used to treat agitation and aggression, along with the level of evidence that supports their use. Specifically, Guideline 5 suggests when to medicate, duration of therapy, failed trials, and how and when to add another agent. The recommendations in the guidelines are based on symptom severity and are consensus-based.[25] Note that no drugs are approved for treatment of aggression, and few controlled studies provide evidence of efficacy for various agents in elders.[25,26]

DRUG-INDUCED COGNITIVE IMPAIRMENT

Medications account for up to 39 percent of the causes of reversible delirium.[27] Furthermore, 5 to 12 percent of suspected cases of dementia are drug-induced.[16,28] Polypharmacy and polymedicine increase the relative odds of cognitive impairment: taking four to five medications creates odds of 9.3:1.[29,30]

Consider the possibility of drug-induced cognitive changes whenever patients' cognitive symptoms suddenly worsen, even in patients who already suffer from dementia. Check recent medication changes, as drug-induced cognitive disturbances tend to be dose-related.[29] Drug-induced cognitive impairment is easily confused with other symptoms, especially in seniors with preexisting neurodegenerative disorders.

Numerous drugs are associated with cognitive changes in the elderly. They are shown in the following list:

Acyclovir	Digitalis glycosides	Pergolide
Anticholinergics	Disulfiram	Phenylpropanolamine
Anticonvulsants	Dronabinol	Pilocarpine
Asparaginase	Ganciclovir	Propafenone
Atropine	Histamine-2	Quinidine
Baclofen	antagonists	Salicylates
Barbiturates	Ifosfamide	Seligiline
Benzodiazepines	Interleukin-2	Sulfonamides
Beta-blockers	Ketamine	Trazodone
Buspirone	Levodopa	Tricyclic antidepressants
Caffeine	Maprotiline	Trimethoprim-
Chlorambucil	Mefloquine	sulfamethoxazolen[31]
Chloroquine	Methyldopa	
Clonidine	Methylphenidate	
Clozapine	Metrizamide	
Cytarabine	Metronidazole	

Many of these medications appear on the Beers Criteria for Potentially Inappropriate Medication Use in Older Adults,[32] a document that should be part of every pharmacist's reading and reference material.

CONCLUSION

Cognitive research findings can help pharmacists understand how to deal appropriately with seniors who are experiencing cognitive decline, and with the families who must ultimately make decisions about their care. New research is testing various instructional methods for elders, as well as "brain exercises" that may promote sharp, efficient cognitive skills (see Exhibit 10.4). Many praise the routine

EXHIBIT 10.4.
Cutting Edge: Use It or Lose It

PET scans show that various areas of the brain are activated when the brain is exercised.[a] Conversely, failure to engage the brain creates a very flat PET scan. Many studies have been conducted showing that when people engage in a variety of mentally challenging activities, they can improve or maintain cognitive function. This finding applies to older people as well as young.[b-f] Controlled studies have also shown that individuals do not need professional guidance to reap benefits from brain exercises.[e]

Basically, the goal is to address all seven areas of human intelligence (linguistic skill, musical, logical-math, spatial, bodily kinesthetic, interpersonal/intrapersonal, and insight). Brain exercises work best when every area of the brain is engaged and when areas that are used often are activated in new and different ways. Using the five senses innovatively capitalizes on the brain's natural ability to form associations between different types of information. Unfortunately, no solid research suggests an exact brain workout, and the optimal duration and number of "reps" for these exercises are also unclear. But researchers do know that engaging in linguistic, mathematical, spatial, and physical tasks often decreases the likelihood of dementia and memory problems.

Many brain exercises can be incorporated in a routine easily (although initially, the exercises themselves are not easy). They can be enjoyable, too.

- Dress with your eyes closed.
- Share a silent meal, using only visual cues and gestures to communicate.
- Balance your checkbook without a calculator.
- Break routines: Go to a familiar place via a new route; eat or brush your teeth with your nondominant hand, shop at new grocery store.
- Do crossword puzzles.
- Play a musical instrument (and learn more than just "Michael Row the Boat Ashore"; advance to more complicated music).
- Read copiously and introduce variety into your selection of topics.
- Concentrate and pay attention.
- Tell jokes and stories that force you to think a few lines ahead while you are talking.
- Avoid excessive alcohol and reduce stress in your life.

(continued)

(continued)

- Engage in different types of exercise: walk in a stimulating environment, dance, take a class.

[a]Post SG. Key issues in the ethics of dementia care. *Neurol Clin.* 2000;18:1011-1022.

[b]Wetzel KC, Harmeyer KM. *Mind Games: The Aging Brain and How to Keep It Healthy.* Albany, NY: Thomson Delmar Learning, 2000.

[c]Willis SL, Schaie KW. Training the elderly on the ability factors of spatial orientation and inductive reasoning. *Psychol Aging.* 1986;1:239-247.

[d]Ball K, Berch DB, Helmers KF, et al. Effects of cognitive training interventions with older adults: A randomized controlled trial. Advanced Cognitive Training for Independent and Vital Elderly Study Group. *JAMA* 2002;288:2271-2281.

[e]Fernandez-Ballesteros R, Calero MD. Training effects on intelligence of older persons. *Arch Gerontol Geriatr.* 1995;20:135-148.

[f]Baltes PB, Sowarka D, Kliegl R. Cognitive training research on fluid intelligence in old age: What can older adults achieve by themselves? *Psychol Aging.*1989;4:217-221.

performance of systematic, thought-provoking tasks (e.g., solving the daily crossword puzzle) throughout one's life as memory preservers. The premise "use it or lose it" no longer pertains to just muscle endurance.

***

The Bum's Rush

- *Have you read Nicholas Sparks's* The Notebook*? More than just a romantic little novel, this book describes the feelings an older man experiences when his one great love develops Alzheimer's disease and forgets him.*
- *If a love story doesn't interest you, perhaps G.H. Ephron's series about a neuropsychologist who works on a dementia unit at a psychiatric hospital might. Try* Addiction, Amnesia, Delusion, Guilt *or* Obsessed, *and read carefully to see fine examples of geropsychiatry.*
- *Prefer the hard stuff or history? Try: Stroop JR. Studies of Interference in Serial Verbal Reactions. Journal of Experimental Psychology. 1935;18:643-62.*

NOTES

1. Neisser U. *Cognitive Psychology.* New York: Meredith Publishing; 1967.

2. Ratey JJ. *A User's Guide to the Brain.* New York: Random House, Inc.; 2001.

3. Gardner H. *The Mind's New Science.* New York: Basic Books; 1997.

4. Miller GA. The magical number seven, plus or minus two: Some limits on our capacity for processing information. *Psychol Rev.* 1996;63:81-97.

5. Kurland M, Lupoff R. *The Complete Idiot's Guide to Improving Your Memory.* New York: Macmillan, Inc.; 1999.

6. Shimamura AP. What is metacognition? The brain knows. *Am J Psychol.* 2000;113:142-145.

7. University of Pennsylvania. The Head Injury Center. Cognition, memory and brain injury. Philadelphia, PA: UPENN; 2004. Available at http://www.uphs.upenn.edu/tbilab/recognition/cognition_fxn.shtml. Accessed January 15, 2004.

8. Haan MN, Shemanski L, Jagust WJ, et al. The role of APOE4 in modulating effects of other risk factors for cognitive decline in elderly persons. *JAMA* 1999; 281:40-46.

9. Burke DM. Language, aging and inhibitory deficits: Evaluation of a theory. *Journal of Gerontology: Psychological Sciences* 1997;52:254-264.

10. Burke DM, Harrold RM. Automatic and effortful semantic processes in old age: Experimental and naturalistic approaches. In LL Light and DM Burke (eds.). *Language, Memory and Aging.* New York: Cambridge University Press; 1988.

11. Light LL, Anderson PA. Comprehension of pragmatic implications in young and older adults. In LL Light and DM Burke. (eds.). *Language, Memory and Aging.* New York: Cambridge University Press; 1988.

12. Westerman SJ, Davies G, Glendon IA, Stammers RB, Matthews G. Ageing and word processing competence: Compensation or compilation. *Br J Psychol.* 1998;89:579-597.

13. Johnson EE. Transportation mobility and older drivers. *J Gerontol Nurs.* 2003;29:34-41.

14. Peterson RC, Doody R, Kurz A, et al. Current concepts in cognitive impairment. *Arch Neurol.* 1987;58:1985-1992.

15. U.S. National Institute of Aging. Alzheimer's disease progress report, 2001-2002. Bethesda, MD: NIH; 2003. Available at http://www.alzheimers.org. Accessed January 15, 2004.

16. Lisi DM. Definition of drug-induced cognitive impairment in the elderly. Medscape Pharmacotherapy; 2000;2. Available at www.medscape.com. Accessed January 15, 2004.

17. Roman GC. Facts, myths, and controversies in vascular dementia. *J Neurol Sci.* 2004;226:49-52.

18. Groth-Marnet G. *Handbook of Psychological Assessment.* New York: John Wiley and Sons, Inc; 1997.

19. Folstein MF, Folstein SE, McHugh PR. Mini-Mental State Examination (MMSE). Lutz, FL: Psychological Assessment Resources, Inc.; 1975-2000.

20. Sherman C. Agitation, aggression demand clinical acumen: Practical psychopharmacology: What experts say to do before study results are in. *Clinical Psychiatry News* 2001;29:20.

21. Raskind MA. Evaluation and management of aggressive behavior in the elderly demented patient. *J Clin Psychiatry.* 1999; 15(60 Suppl.):45-49.

22. Mintzer J, Brawman-Mintzer, O. Agitation as a possible expression of generalized anxiety disorder in demented elderly patients: Toward a treatment approach. *J Clin Psychiatry* 1996;57(suppl 7):55-63.

23. Corrigan PW, Yudofsky SC, Silver, JM. Pharmacological and behavioral treatments for aggressive psychiatric inpatients. *Hospital and Community Psychiatry* 1996;44(2):125-133.

24. Shah A, Evans H, Parkash N. Evaluation of three aggression/agitation behaviour rating scales for use on an acute admission and assessment psychogeriatric ward. *Int J Geriatr Psychiatry* 1998;13:415-420.

25. Alexopoulos GS, Silver JM, Kahn DA, Frances A, Carpenter D. (eds.). *The Expert Consensus Guideline Series: Agitation in Older Persons with Dementia.* A Postgraduate Medicine Special Report. New York: The McGraw-Hill Companies, Inc.; 1988.

26. Fleminger S, Greenwood RJ, Oliver DL. Pharmacological management for agitation and aggression in people with acquired brain injury. *Cochrane Database Syst Rev.* 2003;(1):CD003299.

27. Inouye SK. The dilemma of delirium: Clinical and research controversies regarding diagnosis and evaluation of delirium in hospitalized elderly medical patients. *Am J Med.* 1994;97:278-288.

28. Larson EB, Reifler BV, Sumi SM, et al. Diagnostic evaluation of 200 elderly outpatients with suspected dementia. *J Gerontol.* 1985;40:536-543.

29. Moore AR, O'Keefe TO. Drug-induced cognitive impairment in the elderly. *Drugs Aging* 1999;15:15-28.

30. Larson EB, Kukull WA, Buchner D, Reifler BV. Adverse drug reactions associated with global cognitive impairment in elderly persons. *Ann Intern Med.* 1987; 107:169-173.

31. Some drugs that cause psychiatric symptoms. *Med Lett.* 1998; 40:21-25.

32. Fick DW, Cooper JW, Wade WE, et al. Updating the Beers criteria for potentially inappropriate medication use in older adults; Results of a US consensus panel of experts. *Arch Intern Med.* 2003;163:2716-2724.

Chapter 11

Death, the Great Equalizer

An elderly man lay dying in his bed. In death's grip, he suddenly smelled his favorite chocolate chip cookies. Gathering his remaining strength, he pulled himself up and teetered out of the bedroom. With heroic effort, he inched downstairs. Laboring to breathe, he leaned against the doorway, gazing into the kitchen.

He gazed at dozens of cookie racks, hundreds of cookies on the kitchen table and counters. In his delirium he wondered: Was it heaven, or his devoted wife's final act of love? He staggered toward the table, falling to his knees. Anticipating melting chocolate and gooey dough, he reached for a rack. Suddenly his spatula-wielding wife whacked his hand. "Stay out of those," she said. "They're for the funeral."

This story, cute (and macabre) as it is, speaks of the three aspects of death that clinicians often deal with: the patient's dying process and caregiver's concerns, death itself, and the things that need to be done afterward. What might a pharmacist need to know?

END-OF-LIFE CARE

Once it appears that healing is impossible and death is inevitable, many people choose hospice care (see Exhibit 11.1). Hospice employs intensive palliative care steps that do not prolong dying. In the United States, 3,200 hospice programs admit only patients with end-stage illness and survival expectancy of less than six months. Hospice's four care levels—routine home care, continuous home care, inpatient, and family respite services—seek to improve comfort and

Pharmacy Practice in an Aging Society
© 2006 by The Haworth Press, Inc. All rights reserved.
doi:10.1300/5404_11

EXHIBIT 11.1.
Then and Now: Hospice Care

- The demand for hospice continues to grow: 950,000 people received hospice care in 2003, up from 540,000 in 1998 and only approximately 32,000 in 1991.
- Hospice care is provided in approximately 25 percent of deaths.
- Common diagnoses for hospice patients include cancer (49.0 percent), end-stage heart disease (11.0 percent), dementia (9.6 percent), lung disease (6.8 percent), and kidney disease (2.8 percent).
- The average length of stay is fifty-five days, although 35 percent of patients die within the first seven days in hospice.
- Some 54 percent of hospice patients are women.
- Hospice serves people of all ages, but 63 percent are older than seventy-five.
- Hospice care is most frequently provided in a home setting (95.5 percent).

Sources: National Hospice and Palliative Care Organization. *NHPCO facts and figures.* Alexandria, VA: NHPCO; 2006. Available at www .nhpco.org/templates/1/homepage.cfm (accessed December 12, 2004). Hospice Foundation of America. *What is hospice?* Washington DC: Hospice Foundation of America; 2006 Available at www. hospice foundation.org. Accessed December 2004; Centers for Disease Control and Prevention. *Hospice and Home Health Agency Characteristics: 1991.* Atlanta GA: CDC; 1991 Available at www.cdc.gov/nchs/data/ series/sr_13/sr13_120.pdf. Accessed September 2004.

quality of life for the patient at life's end, and for caregivers after their loved one dies.

Pharmacists need to be familiar with the five rules guiding hospice care:

1. Identify all symptoms.
2. Limit procedures to those that improve quality of life and ameliorate suffering.
3. Use rapid interventions.
4. Provide care and intervene expeditiously.
5. Prescribe treatments free from marked adverse effects or complex monitoring and administration requirements.[1]

Hospice pharmacy is patient driven; patients and their loved ones actively participate in treatment decisions. Patients' mercurial symptom clusters often include pain, weakness, dyspnea, anorexia, constipation, early satiety, fatigue, and dry mouth.[2,3] Palliative treatment and imminent death require creative, aggressive medication regimens using FDA-approved drugs for any reasonable purpose.[3] Clinicians try to treat symptoms without medication, adjust a patient's current medications to relieve new symptoms, or if death is near, avoid additional medication entirely.

Pain

Hospice providers manage pain aggressively, supported by state and federal patients' rights laws mandating effective pain management.[4] Even international groups such as the World Health Organization (WHO) have addressed this issues. The three steps of the WHO analgesic ladder (Figure 11.1) provide relief for 70 percent of patients.[5,6] The WHO and hospice mantra concerning pain relief is simple enough; they apply five essential concepts for drug therapy of cancer pain:

1. By the mouth
2. By the clock
3. By the ladder
4. For the individual
5. With attention to detail

Although hypotension, decreased respiratory rate, and/or altered consciousness are associated with opioid use, hospice uses optimal comfort, as defined and controlled by the patient, as the sole measure of success. Hospice providers prefer oral administration—needlesticks are avoided—but never deny access to medication (and neither should you).[3] Radiation therapy is used to relieve localized bone pain,[6,7] and adjunctive agents (antidepressants, anticonvulsants) help manage other symptoms.[8]

Pain and other symptoms may cause patients to ask for rapid death.[9] In rare circumstances, the American Academy of Pain Medi-

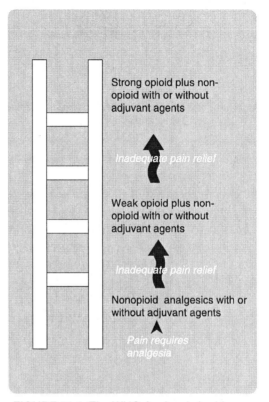

FIGURE 11.1. The WHO Analgesic Ladder

cine's position allows therapeutic and medically appropriate sedation for intractable pain and suffering if the patient requests it.[10] (See Exhibit 11.2.)

Intractable pain is a large issue that includes the assisted suicide referenda, ethical considerations of euthanasia, and the like. "The Bum's Rush" at the end of this chapter provides additional reading suggestions germane to these topics.

Fluid Balance

Fluid imbalance and edema often follow end-stage intravascular problems, nausea, or vomiting. Rehydration therapy can exacerbate

EXHIBIT 11.2.
Quality Care at the End of Life:
A Position Statement from the
American Academy of Pain Medicine

Effective pain and symptom management is an ethical obligation for all health care providers and organizations. Fostering effective pain management at the end of life requires the understanding that such care may prolong life, even though these efforts to relieve pain at times may be perceived as hastening death. In all instances where the primary intent of therapeutic interventions is to alleviate pain and suffering and not to cause death, aggressive pain management is ethical and appropriate. No obstacles should be placed in the way of providing this care. In rare circumstances, when pain and suffering are resistant to treatment, sedation may be therapeutic and medically appropriate to obtain relief if consistent with the express wishes of the patient.

Patients, families, caregivers, and physicians continue to struggle with the task of caring for the dying and how best to relieve their suffering. The debate on the moral and medical challenges of care for the dying requires a response. That response demands extraordinary efforts to improve end-of-life care and optimal management of pain and suffering. We have the knowledge and ability to deliver skillful and effective control of pain and suffering at the end of life.

This statement was prepared by the following AAPM Quality of Care at the End of Life Committee members: Gerald M. Aronoff, MD (Chair); John Banja, PhD; Marshall Bedder, MD FRCP (C); Kerry W. Cranmer, MD CMD; Rollin M. Gallagher, MD MPH; Sandra H. Johnson, JD LL M; Timothy J. Keay, MD MA-Th; and Joel R. Saper, MD.

Approved by the AAPM Board of Directors on February 12, 1998.

edema and contribute to skin breakdown.[8] Hospice nurses provide meticulous mouth care (sometimes with hydrogen peroxide or KY Jelly) or offer sips of liquid or ice chips as alternatives to intravenous (IV) therapy.[8] Sometimes, however, IV hydration can hasten excretion of drug metabolites and provide relief.[7]

Delirium

Delirium may be drug- or drug withdrawal-induced, or it may be a consequence of dyspnea, hepatic insufficiency, vitamin deficiencies, or hypoalbuminemia.[2,11] Haloperidol, risperidol, olanzapine, or lorazepam are often helpful. Clinicians prefer the more sedating neuroleptics for bedridden patients.[7] (See Chapter 10 for more information on delirium.)

Cachexia

Different conditions have different propensities toward cachexia (profound weight loss and emaciation occurring in the course of a chronic disease); for example, lung cancer and AIDS often lead to cachexia, but breast cancer rarely does. Poor appetite, muscle wasting, and altered metabolism respond poorly to nutritional and parenteral nutrition interventions.[2,12,13] Clinicians may prescribe drugs that increase protein synthesis and decrease proteolysis, including gemcitabine, corticosteroids (which improve anorexia but not cachexia), progestin (coupled with exercise), or thalidomide.[8] Thalidomide may also lessen insomnia, pain, nausea, and profuse sweating.[14]

Other Symptoms

The constellation of symptoms people experience toward the end of life varies. Symptoms are often iatrogenic. Constipation, diarrhea, skin breakdown, infections, and weakened immunity frequently beset the dying patient. So do anger, depression, and anxiety. Anxiolytics and antidepressants can help, but fast onset of action is imperative. For this reason, clinicians often prefer methylphenidate (which can also improve fatigue[15,16]) over agents that require weeks to work.[8] See Exhibit 11.3 for communication tips to deal with elders who have concerns at end of life.

AUTOPSY

After death, the deceased's loved ones sometimes consider, or are asked to authorize, an autopsy. The word's Greek origin ("to see with one's eyes") reflects the fact that, until fairly recently, autopsy find-

EXHIBIT 11.3. *Communication:* End-of-life Communication—Dyspnea

Mr. Ellsworth visits the pharmacy late one afternoon and is distraught about his wife, who is near death from metastatic breast cancer. He tells you that she can't catch her breath, and that he thinks the doctors should give her oxygen. Your answer?

Good: Express empathy and explain that many (70 percent) of patients with terminal illnesses experience frightening labored breathing, breathlessness, and gasping. These symptoms suggest hypoxia (lack of oxygen), but most hospice patients are not hypoxic.[a,b,c] The symptoms frequently frighten patients and their loved ones.

Better: Go on to say that pulmonary edema and respiratory failure (fluid in the lungs or lung failure), obstruction anemia (loss of iron in the blood), electrolyte imbalance (changes in blood composition), cardiac decompensation (poor heart function), anxiety, and lymphangitis (inflammation of the lymph glands) may be the cause.

Best: Say, "Supplemental oxygen may not help, Mr. Ellsworth. What have the doctors told you about underlying causes? Are they correcting them?" Use his name so you keep his attention. Advise keeping her room cool, trying stress management techniques, and helping her relax. Know that low-dose opioids and anxiolytics (usually benzodiazepines) can help; call the physician in the rare case that these are not being used.[a,b,c] Recent research has demonstrated that morphine can successfully lessen dyspnea, either orally or by nebulizer (using the IV formulation mixed with saline), and, used carefully, does not cause respiratory depression.[d,c] Managing the dyspneic, frail elderly patient requires a shift from "start low and go slow" to "aggressively titrate as needed but no further" to meet the patient's needs and avoid side effects.[e]

[a]Booth S, Kelly MJ, Cox NP, Adams L, Guz A. Does oxygen help dyspnea in patients with cancer? *Am J Respir Crit Care Med.* 1996; 153:1515-1518.

[b]Mazzocato C, Buclin T, Rapin CH. The effects of morphine on dyspnea and ventilatory function in elderly patients with advanced cancer: A randomized double-blind controlled trial. *Ann Oncol.* 1999;10:1511-1514.

[c]Bruera E, Sweeney C, Willey J, et al. A randomized controlled trial of supplemental oxygen versus air in cancer patients with dyspnea. *Palliat Med.* 2003;17:659-663.

[d]Mazzocato C, Buclin T, Rapin CH. The effects of morphine on dyspnea and ventilatory function in elderly patients with advanced cancer: A randomized double-blind controlled trial. *Ann Oncol.* 1999;10:1511-1514.

[e]Stein WM, Min YI. Nebulized morphine for paroxysmal cough and dyspnea in a nursing home resident with metastatic cancer. *Am J Hosp Palliat Care.* 1997;14:52-56.

ings were limited to what could be seen by the naked eye. Today, pathologists augment vision with technology. Clinicians, researchers, toxicologists, regulators, and legislators use autopsy findings for reasons as diverse as identifying medication error, developing new labeling, or implementing stricter laws. Hospital (or clinical or academic) autopsies are requested or performed by hospital staff to learn more about a patient's illness and treatment, or as a quality improvement tool. They require family consent.[17]

Forensic autopsies address legal and judicial concerns about the circumstances surrounding a person's death, clarifying both the cause (e.g., acute respiratory failure) and the manner of death (e.g., suicide from self-administered drug overdose). Legal entities like the coroner (an elected official) or state medical examiner (an appointed official) perform forensic autopsies; family consent is unnecessary.[17]

Rapid autopsies are used as an alternative to aborted fetal tissue to harvest stem cells from adults after death. Astrocytes, microglia, and neurons harvested from even the very old are in excellent condition at the time of death.[18] Rapid autopsy is also used to salvage organs for transplant.[17] Exhibit 11.4 covers questions families ask frequently when autopsy is a possibility.

Autopsy Procedures

A complete autopsy examines the entire body; no part is off-limits. A limited autopsy, on the other hand, examines a single body part (e.g., the kidneys) or a specific region (e.g., the abdomen). Sometimes, families exclude certain organs from the procedure (e.g., the brain), or the medical examiner or pathologist may believe that only one area of the body requires investigation. Some argue, however, that limited autopsies limit answers.[19] Complete autopsy affords the best confirmation of possible drug involvement, and takes two to three hours, with a final report completed within thirty days.[20] Exhibit 11.5 describes autopsy trends over the ages.

Payment Issues

The average autopsy costs between $500 and $3,500, depending on its type and associated laboratory tests.[21] The jurisdiction where

EXHIBIT 11.4.
Communication: Questions Families Frequently
Ask About Autopsy

What can autopsy identify?

Autopsies can reveal how a relative died, medical error(s), hereditary illness, or whether the deceased's problem was contagious.[a]

After the autopsy, is the whole body returned?

The specific autopsy consent form has the answer. Some institutions return organs to the body cavity; others incinerate them. Some save tissues for research or teaching.[b]

Do the major religions forbid autopsy?

Christianity, Islam, and Judaism do not absolutely forbid autopsy, and Hinduism permits respectful autopsy.[c] Leonardo da Vinci received papal approval to perform more than thirty dissections, and in the 15th century, Pope Sixtus IV allowed human dissection in Bologna and Padua. In 1952, the leader of the Islamic School of Jurisprudence sanctioned autopsies to investigate unnatural deaths. Reform Judaism permits autopsies that increase medical understanding.[c]

When is the corpse embalmed?

Usually, after the autopsy. If the deceased had a known infectious illness, embalming may be done before.

Can we have an open casket after an autopsy?

Generally, the pathologist releases the body shortly after the autopsy, but may keep the organs. The incisions on the cadaver cannot be seen when the body is presented for viewing.

Are any drugs undetectable in overdose?

As recently as 1979 pharmacy students were taught that insulin, digitalis, succinyl choline, and potassium were undetectable, and hence, instruments of the perfect crime. With rare exceptions, modern toxicologic assays can identify almost any drug remaining in body tissues.[d]

(continued)

(continued)

If the family wants an autopsy, but the hospital refuses, what recourse is available?

Although not legally obligated to conduct autopsies, some hospitals charge families for autopsy. Others may refuse to do the autopsy, sometimes as a legal maneuver.[b] (More often than not, autopsy reveals that suspicious deaths were due to natural causes.[e,f])Families can hire private companies and independent pathologists to perform the autopsy (call 1-800-autopsy, or search the Internet using the term "private autopsy"), order tests, and report the findings to the family.

[a]Oppewal F, Meyboom-de Jong B. Family members' experience of autopsy. *Fam Pract.* 2001;18(3):304-308.

[b]Hanzlick R, Mosunjac MI. The rest of the story. *Arch Intern Med.* 1999;159(11):1173-1176.

[c]Davis GJ, Peterson BR. Dilemmas and solutions for the pathologist and clinician encountering religious views of the autopsy. *South Med J.* 1996; 89(11):1041-1044.

[d]DiMaio VJ, DiMaio D. *Forensic Pathology. 2nd Edition.* Boca Raton: CRC Press; 2001.

[e]Webster JR, Derman D, Kopin J, et al. Obtaining permission for an autopsy: Its importance for patients and physicians. *A J of Med.* 1989; 86(3):325-326.

[f]Brody JE. A price to pay as autopsies lose favor. *NY Times* News Service. January 9, 2001. Available at http://partners.nytimes.com/library/national/science/health/hth-col-index.html. Accessed December 14, 2004.

the death occurred pays for forensic autopsies. Because autopsy is not considered a therapeutic intervention, government and private insurers generally will not pay. When a hospital orders an autopsy, the hospital absorbs the costs. Medicare allows hospitals to include autopsy overhead costs in the reimbursement rates they set.

Determining Drug Use or Abuse Postmortem

The manner of death—natural, suicide, accidental, homicide, and undetermined—often involves drugs.[17] Sometimes called the "three curses," alcohol, morphine, and cocaine have been implicated in in-

EXHIBIT 11.5.
Then and Now: Autopsy Trends

Autopsy rates have steadily declined from approximately 50 percent in the 1940s to between 10 percent and 15 percent in 1985.[a] From 1986 through 1995, annual inpatient deaths remained constant, but autopsy rates declined further to 7 percent.[b] For years, the National Center for Health Statistics collected national autopsy data, but in 1995 they stopped. Independent researchers continued to watch, however, and one study documents continued decline from 1995 through 1997.[c] A recent survey found that half of 244 hospitals autopsied at rates of below 9 percent[b] and some hospitals have not conducted autopsies in years.[d] Even with internal medicine residency accreditation requiring a 15 percent autopsy rate, some teaching hospitals report a rate of 2 percent to 3 percent.[d,e]

Fewer autopsies are performed on the elderly than on the young.[a] And although the hospital autopsy rate has fallen, autopsy rates for unnatural deaths have remained relatively stable.[c] Public disinclination is not the cause: 68 percent of the public have no personal objections to autopsy.[f]

Numerous factors have contributed to the decline in autopsy rates, including[a,c,g,h]

- insurer and Medicare refusal to pay for autopsy;
- misperception that advanced technologic and diagnostic procedures are more accurate and can replace autopsy;
- fear of litigation following discovery of diagnostic errors or imprudent treatment decisions;
- the time-consuming nature of obtaining consent;
- medical schools' departure from anatomical dissection toward computerized learning aids;
- autopsies' cumbersome procedures needed/mandated to prevent the spread of pathogens or other contaminants during autopsy, combined with increasing awareness of the risk of infectious diseases; and
- the elimination by the Joint Commission on Accreditation of Healthcare Organizations of minimum mandatory autopsy rates as an accreditation requirement.

[a]Dessmon HY, El-Bilbeisi H, Tewari S, et al. A study of consecutive autopsies in a medical ICU: A comparison of clinical cause of death and autopsy diagnosis. *Chest.* 2001;119:530-536.

[b]Hanzlick R, Baker P. Institutional autopsy rates. *Arch Intern Med.* 1998;158(11):1171-1172.

(continued)

(continued)

cBurton EC, Nemetz PN. Medical error and outcomes measures: Where have all the autopsies gone? *Medscape General Medicine* 2000; 2(2). Available at www.medscape.com Accessed June 6, 2002.

dThe importance of an autopsy. Available at http://dying.about.com/library/weekly/aa061399.htm Accessed June 6, 2002).

eLandefeld CS, Chren MM, Myers A, et al. Diagnosis yield of the autopsy in a university hospital and a community hospital. *N Engl J Med.* 1988;318:1249-1254.

fBurton EC, Nemetz PN. Institutional and economic influences on autopsy performance – in reply. *Medscape General Medicine* 2(3), 2000. Available at www.medscape.com. Accessed June 2002.

gRoosen HJ, Frans E, Wilmer A, et al. Comparison of premortem clinical diagnoses in critically ill patients and subsequent autopsy findings. *Mayo Clin Proc.* 2000;75:562-567.

hGregory SR, Cole TR. The changing role of dissection in medical education. *MSJAMA* 2002;287:1180-1181. Available at www.ama-assn.org/sci-pubs/msjama/articles. Accessed June 6, 2002.

numerable drug-related deaths throughout history and these drugs continue to be implicated today.[22] To determine the manner of death, the medical examiner looks at toxicology test results, the deceased's medical history, autopsy findings, and the circumstances leading to death.[22] Today, fewer than 1 percent of autopsies lead to a finding of "undetermined."

When authorities suspect drugs may have precipitated or hastened death, they have several recourses. Toxicology screening can be performed on blood, vitreous humor, tissue, muscle, hair, fingernails, or urine. Specific tests look for ethanol, acidic and neutral drugs, basic compounds, narcotics, volatiles, and cannabis.[17,22] When bodies in various states of decomposition challenge the pathologist, the predictable cycles of invasion by green flies, maggots, beetles, spiders, mites, and millipedes may offer clues. Because these parasites consume not only the body but also the substances in the tissues, pathologists can analyze the actual insects to determine whether an overdose or poisoning may have occurred.[17,22]

Autopsy is not an exact science. If the deceased lived for several days after ingesting a fatal drug dose, all of the drug might have been metabolized. If the deceased was hospitalized or had lab work done recently, antemortem samples may still be available for comparison. Some drugs redistribute after death causing misleading levels. Finally, drug tolerance differs widely among individuals—a level that is fatal in one person may not be so in another.[22]

Accidental Death

All drugs are poisons and all poisons are drugs.[23] Frequently, medications, home remedies, illicit drugs, or alcohol are implicated in accidental death. Half of all motor vehicle accidents involve alcohol. Autopsy pathologists look for alcohol blood levels, and also use vitreous ethanol levels; if for some reason no blood is available for analysis, vitreous fluid can be used. A vitreous fluid alcohol level is 1.2 times what would have been identified in the blood, so the pathologist can extrapolate the blood alcohol level. They also look at the pancreas and liver for signs of chronic alcohol use.[22,23] Pathologists take samples of all tissues and body fluids when it seems as if death was accidental, looking for an accumulation of any drug or poison that may have caused the mishap.

Suicide

Drugs are second only to guns as tools of suicide. The tricyclic antidepressants are used most often, but other drugs and mixed-drug suicides are also common. Because the tricyclics may redistribute after death, vitreous levels, stomach contents, and evidence such as empty vials and prescription records become important. Any drug with a narrow therapeutic index can cause death quickly, but even those that are fairly safe become perilous when combined with other drugs, such as alcohol and benzodiazepines.[22,23]

Homicide

People do occasionally use drugs to kill others, less successfully than in years past. Drugs that used to be undetectable (insulin, digitalis, succinyl choline, and potassium) can no longer elude modern technology. Gas chromatography-mass spectrometry and chemiluminescent radioimmunoassay detect the first three, even after embalming.[23] Potassium poisoning is difficult to detect, but investigation, confession, and finding of paraphernalia often crack the case. A needle mark or subtle discoloration in soft tissue may have high potassium levels, compared with control samples on the contralateral side of the body.[24] When foul play is suspected, pathologists will augment the visible with toxicology findings and other evidence to determine cause of death.

Natural Death

Autopsy can reveal valuable information even when the death is clearly a natural one, such as the cardiac patient who has a final heart attack or the cancer victim who succumbs to her disease. The pathologist's findings may prove educational or lifesaving for others. Even if drugs are not implicated in a death, pathologists find evidence indicating that people used over-the-counter, prescription, or illicit drugs during their lives, which may heighten awareness of such abuses in the community and energize public campaigns. For example, cascara laxatives cause melanosis coli pigment, a brownish black colon discoloration, and minocycline partitions into the thyroid.[23] One study autopsied 234 nursing home patients and found an 8 percent incidence of previously undiagnosed pulmonary embolism. Venous thromboembolic disease was the most frequently missed diagnosis among these patients, a finding that reinforces the fact that clinically silent conditions can cause significant mortality.[25] Regardless of the manner of death, the deceased's complete medical history explains unusual pathological changes, even if they were peripheral to the real cause of death. Several studies reiterate that sophisticated diagnostic techniques (e.g., imaging techniques, molecular biological assays, and biopsy techniques) do not always provide accurate information.[26-29]

Although not performed as often as in the past, autopsies continue to have a vital role in medicine: ascertaining the quality of antemortem care, confirming diagnoses, documenting new diseases, validating the accuracy of medical technology, and teaching and research. Until the concordance between antemortem and postmortem data is near perfect, the autopsy will continue as the gold standard. A popular sign in

many autopsy rooms states "Hic locus est ubi mors gaudet succure vi-
tae"—This is the place where death delights to serve the living.[29]

CLEANING OUT THE MEDICATION CABINET

Almost every pharmacist has this experience at least once: a patient's family asks what they can do with medications after an older
relative dies. Keep in mind that seniors who lived through the Great
Depression often save things, sentimentalize clutter, or are fearful of
throwing anything away lest it be needed "someday."[30] They sometimes have cabinets full of partial bottles, and surviving families or
spouses wonder whether Aunt Sallie can use Daddy's costly medications now that he is gone, or whether flushing drugs down the toilet is
a good idea. What is the most responsible way to dispose of unwanted
drugs?

Most states forbid transfer of prescription medication to other patients for several reasons. Once the prescription leaves the pharmacy,
its storage is in question. Many patients, cleaning out medication cabinets, flush unwanted drugs down the toilet. Or they call their local
waste processor and are given incorrect or inappropriate information.
Calls to waste processors rarely begin with the employee asking,
"What kind of drugs?" They often consider vitamins, controlled substances, monoclonal antibodies, and antineoplastic chemotherapy
identical, and their answers sometimes make little sense.

The U.S. Environmental Protection Agency now discourages flushing medications down the toilet because sewage treatment plants cannot remove pharmaceutical and personal care product (PPCP) residue
from water. Pharmacies, hospitals, and drug manufacturers struggle
with the issue, and indigent or war-torn countries that have received
unsuitable charitable donations do, too. During the Bosnian war, drug
donations often were a mismatch for the country's needs in kind or
quantity, outdated, labeled in languages unknown to Bosnians, or
lacking essential information. Similar problems occur globally in
times of great crisis or need. After Bosnia, the WHO issued drug disposal guidelines.[31] In the United States, each state addresses drug
disposal in its own way, because no federal guideline exists. Some

states ignore the issue entirely.[32] Poisonings, illegal dumping, and detection of PPCPs in water have galvanized discussion.[33]

How big is the problem? In Canada, a hospital advertised that it would collect unwanted and expired medications from surrounding communities. Over two days, they collected 47 kg from twenty-five people.[34] Psychiatric patients sometimes hoard unused medications at home, so a mental health facility in Washington, DC, offered prizes to patients surrendering the most bottles. The winner: an elderly man who delivered 185 prescription vials in garbage bags. Sauntering off with his chocolate-covered cherries, he admitted he had not brought *all* of his old bottles. He saved some just in case the contest became an annual event.

Prevention Is the Best Medicine

Even before someone asks you for advice about a medicine cabinet crammed with drugs, there are steps you can take to minimize the environmental challenge. Environmentally sensitive pharmacies should commit to meeting society's pharmacy needs in ways that do not diminish future generations' environmental capacity. Environmentalists call this "sustainability."[35] Show customers, employees, and stakeholders specific, measurable goals, like doubling the number of pounds of material sent for recycling each month or identifying three "greener" sources for supplies.

Ask pharmaceutical and supply vendors about their environmental policies, signaling that this is one of your purchasing criteria. State your preference for recycled and recyclable materials, and for vendors who agree to give credit for or destroy unused products. Ask vendors to change packages to more appropriate sizes for your elderly clients, improve their packaging, or list recommended disposal routes on their labeling as pesticide manufacturers do.[35] Also, use just-in-time delivery systems so you only receive exactly what you need, when you need it.

At the patient level, environmental concerns are yet another reason to employ the lowest possible dose, use the fewest and, indeed, "cleanest" medications in terms of target symptoms or adverse effects. Discontinue unnecessary drugs.[35] A drug avoided is a drug unexcreted.

Forbid samples, because with their excessive packaging-to-product ratio, they are environmental nightmares. The Canadian hospital mentioned previously found that 87 percent of what they collected were physician's samples.[34] Samples also tend to be stored in areas that are not routinely checked for expired products and to be dispensed without adequate labeling or patient education.

The Thankless Job: The Nitty-Gritty

When the deceased's family members come to you for help, keep in mind that they may be frustrated with the cleaning process, or still in bereavement. Note also that they may have no idea why there are so many medications in the medicine cabinet, or be upset by what they have found there (e.g., a prescription for erectile dysfunction or many opioid analgesics). They may have questions about specific prescriptions, and if you cannot or prefer not to answer them, explain politely that you really do not know what to say, and it is probably best not to second-guess the deceased's motivations for not having shared the information when he or she was alive.

Advise them to take these steps:

1. Sort through the medicine cabinet. Take everything out and separate items into piles—one for items that should remain in the cabinet or will be given to someone else, one for any prescriptions with the deceased person's name on them. Outdated over-the-counter drugs, as well as unused and unneeded items, should go in the latter pile for destruction, too. Open bottles of any liquid that may have been there a while should be discarded; liquid evaporation can concentrate the remaining contents, or some of the drug or excipient may have precipitated. Soiled bottles, items with dry rot . . . If in doubt, throw it out.
2. Identify other areas where the deceased may have stored medications. Check bedside drawers, kitchen cabinets, and refrigerators for collections. Also check the deceased person's old purses on closet shelves, automobile glove compartment (yes, they should not store drugs there, but they do), or tote bags.
3. Incinerate the detritus if the geographic area uses a state-of the-art incineration facility. Tell patients whose communities incinerate

to package drugs carefully, so others are not exposed to the drugs, and put them into the garbage immediately before pickup.

4. If your area does not incinerate, and pharmacies are allowed to take drugs back, and you have access to an incinerator, tell the family that you will dispose of the accumulation for them. Ask them to package the drugs the way you want to receive them to minimize breakage and ensure your staff will not be exposed to anything dangerous.

5. As a last resort, families can use the trash can. Avoid the three problems associated with throwing medications into the trash (safety, abuse, and pollution) using these tips:

   a. Leave medication in its original, child-proof containers or prescription vials labeled with the drug's name, so officials can identify the substance in the event someone finds and ingests it. Remove or obliterate the patient information for privacy.

   b. Adulterate drugs. Dumpster divers will find medications that are mixed with a little water and some kitty litter, flour, or a nontoxic spice (like hot pepper, but not nutmeg which can be toxic in large amounts) unappealing.

   c. Seal the drugs in a brown paper bag or box, and place the package in the trash as close as possible to garbage pickup time.

   d. Be particularly careful with liquids, especially if they are in glass bottles. Seal them into a ziplock bag or a plastic container, so if they break, others will not be exposed.

CONCLUSION

Death and the periods of time that precede and follow it are often accompanied by fear, anxiety, and, unfortunately, aversion and avoidance. Pharmacists who understand and provide sensitive, high-quality end-of-life care become an asset to patients, families, and communities. They will also find that there is a niche for these services, and families welcome their help.

The Bum's Rush

- *Irene Marcuse's mystery novel* Consider the Alternative *describes a neighborhood where several elderly people commit suicide following directions provided in the Hemlock Society's famous guide to death,* Final Exit.

- *Approximately 400,000 volunteers work for hospice, accounting for 10 percent of all hours provided to hospice patients. Look in your area if this is an opportunity that interests you.*
- *Know your state's drug disposal regulations. Generally, states are concerned with safety, but also with controlled substance disposition. Some states prohibit pharmacies from taking back unused drugs from patients, even for destruction. Others have very specific disposal rules, including misguided requirements to flush drugs down a drain. Know yours, and if they aren't "green," write to the state pharmacy board to suggest changes.*
- *The Commonwealth of Virginia provides a list of firms authorized by the Drug Enforcement Administration to destroy controlled substances (www.dhp.state.va.us/pharmacy/guidelines/110-06%20 Destruction%20 of%20Schedule%20II-V%20Drugs. doc) without a witness at the incinerator. Other states probably do, too. Many of the firms listed are reverse distributors that return drugs to manufacturers for pharmacies for a percentage of the credit value or at a per piece rate. These firms document everything carefully and thoroughly and often provide customers with prepaid shipping labels. They incinerate all products that cannot be returned to the manufacturer, and are licensed to accept all expired or otherwise returned drugs. Unmarked items that cannot be identified by a registered pharmacist are treated in a "worst case" way and incinerated as hazardous. If drugs have been removed from the original bottle, manufacturers usually agree to accept the drugs for destruction or allow the reverse distributor to incinerate them. Pharmaceutical manufacturers want to ensure that their products are disposed of properly and will go to great lengths to help. Some reverse distributors will incinerate returned patient medications for free for their customers, since there is no credit value.*

NOTES

1. Terminal care: Not just pain management. *Prescribe Int.* 1998;7:57-63.

2. U.S. National Institutes of Health. Symptoms in terminal illness: A research workshop. Bethesda, MD: NIH; 2001. Available at www.nih.gov/ninr/end-of-life.htm. Accessed April 4, 2001.

3. Joranson DE, Gilson AM. Pharmacists' knowledge of and attitudes toward opioid pain medications in relation to federal and state policies. *J Am Pharm Assoc.* 2001;41:213-220.

4. Consensus statement of the American Academy of Pain Medicine and the American Pain Society. The use of opioids for the treatment of chronic pain. Glenview, IL: Gapm; 1996. Available at www.painmed.org. Accessed January 2004.

5. Jadad AR, Browman G. The WHO analgesic ladder for cancer pain management. *JAMA* 1995;274:1870-1873.

6. Foley K. A 44-year-old woman with severe pain at the end of life. *JAMA* 1999;281:1937-1955.

7. National Comprehensive Cancer Network. Palliative Care Guidelines. Jenkintown, PA: NCCN; 2005. Available at www.nccn.org/physician_gls/PDF/pilliative.pdf. Accessed January 2004.

8. Zanni GR, Wick JY Hospice care: A noble calling for the consultant pharmacist. *The Consultant Pharmacist* 2001;16:821-836.

9. Loewy EH. Terminal sedation, self-starvation, and orchestrating end-of-life. *Arch Intern Med.* 2001;161:329-340.

10. Gapm. Position statement of the American Academy of Pain Medicine. Quality care at the end of life. Glenview, IL: Gapm; 1998. Available at www.painmed.org. Accessed January 15, 2004.

11. Fick DW, Cooper JW, Wade WE, et al. Updating the Beers criteria for potentially inappropriate medication use in older adults; Results of a US consensus panel of experts. *Arch Intern Med.* 2003;163:2716-2724.

12. Pinkowish MD. Management of pain and discomfort. *Patient Care* 2000:34:38-59.

13. Kaplan D. Ethical decision making at the end of life: A series of case studies. *Patient Care* 2000;34:130-140.

14. Peuckmann V, Fisch M, Bruera E. Potential novel uses of thalidomide: Focus on palliative care. *Drugs* 2000:60:273-92.

15. Bruera E, Driver L, Barnes EA, et al. Patient-controlled methylphenidate for the management of fatigue in patients with advanced cancer: A preliminary report. *J Clin Oncol.* 2003;21:4439-4443.

16. Escalante CP. Treatment of cancer-related fatigue: An update. *Support Care Cancer* 2003;11:79-83.

17. Newman J, McLemore. Forensic medicine: Matters of life and death. *Radiol Technol.* 1999;71(2):169-185

18. Meyer JR. Human embryonic stem cells and respect for life. *J Med Ethics.* 2000;26:166-170.

19. Davis GJ, Hanzlick R. A tale of the unexpected: Finding a zebra. *Arch Internal Med.* 1997;157:2296.

20. Hanzlick R, Mosunjac MI. The rest of the story. *Arch Intern Med.* 1999 14;159(11):1173-1176.

21. Burton EC, Nemetz PN. Institutional and economic influences on autopsy performance—in reply. *Medscape General Medicine* 2000;2(3). Available at www.medscape.com. Accessed June 4, 2002.

22. DiMaio VJ, DiMaio D. *Forensic Pathology,* 2nd edition. Boca Raton: CRC Press; 2001.

23. Freidlander E. Ed's Pathology Meltdown. Kansas, MO: 2006. Available at www.pathguy.com. Accessed December 10, 2004.

24. Fierro M, Virginia Department of Health. E-mail correspondence with JY Wick. July 2, 2002.

25. Gross JS, Neufeld RR, Libow LS, Gerber I, Rodstein M. Autopsy study of the elderly institutionalized patient. Review of 234 autopsies. *Arch Intern Med.* 1988; 148:173-176.

26. Dessmon HY, El-Bilbeisi H, Tewari S, et. Al. A study of consecutive autopsies in a medical ICU: A comparison of clinical cause of death and autopsy diagnosis. *Chest* 2001;119:530-536.

27. Hanzlick R, Baker P. Institutional autopsy rates. *Arch Intern Med.* 1998 8;158(11):1171-1172.

28. Landefeld CS, Chren MM, Myers A, et. al. Diagnosis yield of the autopsy in a university hospital and a community hospital. *N Engl J Med.* 1988;318:1249-1254.

29. Roosen HJ, Frans E, Wilmer A, et al. Comparison of premortem clinical diagnoses in critically ill patients and subsequent autopsy findings. *Mayo Clin Proc.* 2000;75:562-567.

30. Zemke R, Raines C, Filipczak B. *Generations at Work: Managing the Clash of Veterans, Boomers, Xers, and Nexters in Your Workplace.* New York: American Management Association; 2000.

31. World Health Organization. Guidelines for the safe disposal of unwanted pharmaceuticals in and after emergencies: Interagency guidelines. Geneva, Switzerland: WHO;1999. Available at http://w3.whosea.org/rdoc/rdoc/publication.asp? bkid=202. Accessed June 9, 2003.

32. Daughton CG, Ternes TA. Pharmaceuticals and personal care products in the environment: Agents of subtle change? *Environ Health Perspect* 1999;6(107 Suppl.):907-938.

33. Birchard K. Out of sight, out of mind . . . the medical waste problem. *Lancet* 2002;359:56.

34. Doucleff M, Terry N. Pumping out the arsenic. *Nat Biotechnol.* 2002; 20:1094-1095.

35. Daughton CG. Cradle-to-cradle stewardship of drugs for minimizing their environmental disposition while promoting human health. I. Rationale for and avenues toward a green pharmacy. *Environ Health Perspect* 2003;111:757-774.

Index